The
Off-season Angler

By

Gary L. Saindon

Foreword by Gary LaFontaine

BOOK DESIGN BY ROBERT A. SAINDON

TO ORDER ADDITIONAL COPIES OF THIS BOOK:
Write Gary Saindon, 2307 Alpine Court, Whitefish, MT 59937 or call
(406) 862-3636.

Published by Gary Saindon, 2307 Alpine Court, Whitefish, MT 59937
Publishing Consultant: Falcon Press Publishing Co., Inc., Billings and Helena,
Montana.
Photos and drawings by Gary Saindon.
Editing and design by Bob Saindon.
Library of Congress Catalog Card Number: 85-90000
ISBN: 0-934318-53-0
Manufactured in the United States of America

Contents

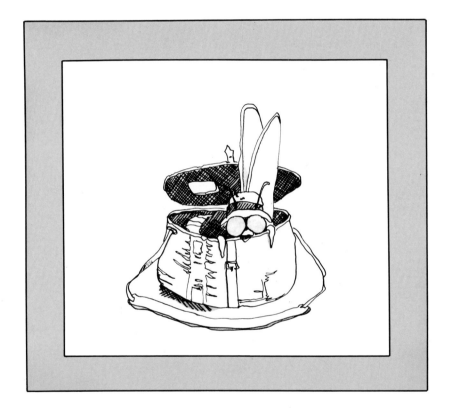

Acknowledgements

Enthusiasm and confidence from a loved one are the forces that bring out labors of love. I have been fortunate to have that support, along with a tolerance for sawdust and feathers from my wife Jayne.

Brother Bobby has really done the toughest part of putting the book together with his artistic and editorial abilities.

Love ya both for helping to transform lumber to projects, and projects to lines and text.

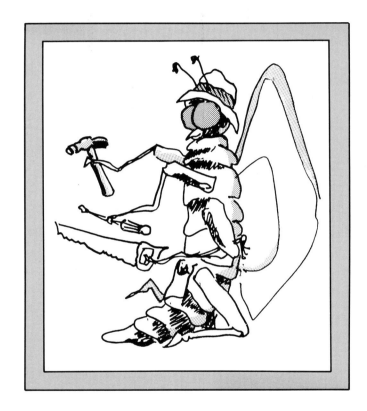

Foreword

It would be hard to imagine anyone better qualified to write a book about woodworking projects for fishermen than Gary Saindon. The author would have to have three talents—woodworking, writing, and fishing (probably in that order of importance)—and there isn't one of these that my friend doesn't do superbly.

We've shared some great fishing trips, on Montana rivers like the Flathead, Smith, and Missouri, and in every angling situation he's demonstrated a tremendous enthusiasm and creativity for problem solving. He thinks out there, always searching for a better, more practical way of achieving a goal.

The writer of this book would have to be a fisherman. How else would he understand the equipment needs of an angler? How else would he test the finished products? Don't be fooled by the beauty of Gary Saindon's wood creations—every one of them is eminently practical. They're tools that make a fishing life not only more fun but more productive.

The author proved to me how well he could write after one of our trips. He did an article for the October 1982 issue of **Flyfishing,** a magazine where his work appears regularly, and he characterized my old fishing truck: ''...rattling up in an old blue pickup that only an experienced mechanic would dare leave home in. The pickup camper, of similar disrepair, seemed to bulge at the corners from the assorted fishing gear visible through the cracked window. The assemblage of expensive equipment was dubiously secured with a battered padlock through a hasp cleverly nailed to a sagging door.''

Now, that's character assassination. Funny, but still an attack on a fly-fishing institution—my beloved old Chevy, the Blue Charm. Anyone who can capture the ambience of the Charm so well has to be a writer, though.

He brings the same wit to his writing in this book. Here is someone like me, not a woodworker (they don't let me shave toothpicks), who totally reveled in **The Off-Season Angler**. The lead-in paragraphs to the various projects have to leave the soberest of people giggling. They're enough to make me want to get out my hammer and screws. This man just has a knack for having fun in everything that he does.

The reader might be misled on the author's woodworking expertise by the text simply because he is so modest. Gary Saindon is a builder, in the best sense of the word, a man who brings craftsmanship to projects big and small. He writes about working on chicken coops; the latest coop he worked on as a builder was the nine million dollar Taj Mahal of Montana, the magnificent Grouse Mountain Lodge in Whitefish. The reader should stop by and see it if he wants to be impressed by how much nine million dollars can buy these days.

To see some of Gary Saindon's smaller projects all I have to do is look in my fishing room. Sitting on the main table is a beautiful Izaak's Desk, his patented fly-tying organizer. It so intelligently stores materials and tools, while providing a work area, that it even keeps me tying efficiently. His wooden fly boxes, as functional as they are beautiful (and worthy of riding in the Blue Charm), store the resulting patterns.

In the end this is a book that transcends its subject because it is so well done. A person doesn't have to be a fisherman or a woodworker to enjoy it. It makes both endeavors sound like so much fun that it will probably inspire some fishermen to try woodworking and some woodworkers to try fishing. And that's the way it should be.

Gary LaFontaine
Deer Lodge, Mt.

The Off-season Angler

With feathers and thread I escape to the dream
Of a trout that was hid 'neath a stump in a stream.
   He's there in the slush of the cold winter's gray
And he waits for the sun.

   I lured him and lied, 'bout the fly I had sent
To his lair in that mine.
   And he took it on faith, the deception not shown
Of the hook and the line.

His anger was wrought, and he thrashed
When he knew of the lie that I sent
With that fly in the foam.

Then he ran when he felt the hook in his jaw
From panic and fright of the angler he saw.
   And he flew to the air.
Then again he was free
To lurk as before, in his home of the stream.

   While winter goes by, I wait, as does he
But I plan and I build a pattern to be
   As real as his food and as strong as his shake
That never comes free, and never will break.

Fisherman/Woodworker

"**A** fly fisherman from necessity," and "a woodworker by choice" have been interchangeable phrases that have continually shifted in priority for me as long as I can remember. The combination of the two captivations probably started when I built a tackle box from a magazine article, (I think it was **Mechanix Illustrated**) when I was in junior high school.

However **you** rate the two priorities, the following projects fit equally well into either. Fishermen who don't work with wood—there must be some—can have the project(s) built; and the woodworker who doesn't fish (probably an agnostic) could build any of them for sale or as gifts.

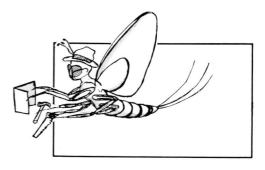

A Philosophy

One percent inspiration is not enough, and ninety-nine percent perspiration is ridiculous. Creativity should account for half of a new project, leaving approximately half for the fun of building it. Besides the original concept, inspiration has to also include leaving your mind receptive to innovations during the progress of construction.

If, for example, you were given an order to build a simple box with a hinged lid measuring 12'' x 6'' x 6'', and no other instructions, you would be forced to make dozens of decisions. If this same order were given to ten other cabinetmakers, the only things the boxes would have in common would be those given in the order (hopefully). Each step of building would require a creative thought on the part of the woodworker.

From the species of wood, through the kind of joints and final finish, you would have to produce creative actions or inspirations.

Over the years, I have had occasions when clients would want something built just because they had one specific need for it. That's usually a pretty good reason. But sometimes a discussion about that need would result in innovations that were more functional, less expensive and usually more pleasant to look at than the original, myopic concept.

Creative woodworking is like creative anything else. Those who work with their tools for a living are selling their time and expertise and are usually forced to work within time (and budget) constraints that limit creativity. Admittedly, there are many carpenters who think the limit of creativity is having a new coffee cup.

But the man who enjoys woodworking as a hobby is in an enviable position. He has the luxury of time. He has the absolute final word in quality control, and an unending innovation budget.

If you are not satisfied with an idea, and that happens many times, don't rush it. I have pursued ideas that didn't start well and they usually got worse. Use the garbage can when you doubt the quality of your work.

But don't hesitate to experiment with different solutions to building problems. I can think of two carpenters that I have known who were creatively lazy. Not lazy creatively. They were both too lazy to accept the hard way that others did things so they would come up with easier and sometimes better ways to accomplish them.

The bottom line is to enjoy your hobby and create the best you can. As the quality of your workmanship improves, enjoy your progress and in the meantime, enjoy your projects.

Not Available In Any Store

This assemblage of projects and fly fishing trivia has evolved from many years of curiosity, frustration, and in some instances an abhorrence for our plastic surroundings. The incongruity of a plastic fishing apparatus against a background of green ferns or wet polished river rock is more than any serious fly fisherman should have to endure. Admittedly, some of the modern synthetics are so far superior to the older materials, that their use is essential to the enjoyment of our sport. The new fly lines and leaders are much better and longer-lasting than the old stuff.

Fly rods of glass, graphite and boron must be accepted for their practicality—the practicality of cost, service and durability. A bad bamboo rod is an abomination. Pretty? Maybe. But I have tried to fish with some of the old rods that would have cast equally well from either end. However, if you are lucky enough to find, or can afford a good bamboo fly rod, don't trade it for a barn full of synthetics.

A bamboo rod, like all contrivances made by hand from natural materials, is one of a kind. If it performs well, it is absolutely precious.

At this point, I must admit to a bit of hypocrisy in my convictions as I do have a modest collection of limited edition bamboo rods that never have, and never will be fished. They are an investment that you could compare with other forms of art work or collectibles that appreciate with time. The difference being that I personally find more beauty in a fine fly rod than in an album filled with stamps.

These projects, when well finished, could be likened to a fine bamboo rod—they will all add to your enjoyment of fly fishing and its related hobbies. I find satisfaction in knowing that the special flies upon which I used my best English hooks and most expensive hackles are safely nestled in fine polished mahogany surroundings.

At my FISHING HEADQUARTERS I am able year 'round to enjoy the pleasures of the many ancillary facets of fly fishing. The long, cold Montana winters are made enjoyable with comfortable fly tying sessions. Reels are dissected for maintenance; rod windings are replaced or recoated; fly lines are cleaned, and leaders are tied.

The FISHING BOX has saved many piscatorial forays for me as well as for others I have fished with. It is a chest for equipment of all kinds—spare equipment, maintenance equipment, safety equipment, and creative equipment in the form of a well-stocked fly-tying kit. Unlike a canvas bag, this box provides real reel protection.

IZAAK'S DESK has a pedigree in the form of a U.S. patent, and was offered for sale by the Orvis Company a few years ago. A high percentage of my fly tying is done at this desk while watching T.V. with the family.

Any of these furnishings, if they were to go through the normal route of manufacture, wholesale and retail, would be quite expensive, and justifiably so. Yet, most people who have even limited shop facilities can build them. If there is a machining procedure that your facilities cannot handle, there are cabinetmaking shops which will spend a few minutes running a molding, or planing stock to a specific thickness. Take the plans to various shops and discuss your needs and the costs involved.

But first ... SAFETY FIRST!

All ''Do It Yourself'' manuals should include references to safety and I don't want to ignore this important part of shop practice. After over twenty-five years of working with tools, I am fortunate to have at least the major portions of all ten fingers; but I have seen accidents that leave me cold just thinking about them.

The most vulnerable period (after proper machine use is learned) is when one is performing repetitious work. Cutting many drawer parts, for example, presents a very dangerous time. The mind loses its focus after the first few passes through the saw, and begins to wander to the next step of construction. Stop the saw occasionally and do something else.

Wear eye protection, sweep the floor often, and be continually conscious of the fact that each time you turn a machine on, it is willing to cut whatever you allow it to cut.

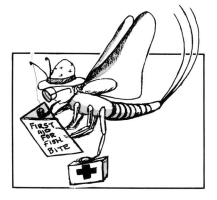

A Fishing Headquarters

Introduction

During the nineteenth century, a typical dentist's office consisted of a small room with a chair and a crude, slow and obviously painful drill. Next to the chair was a cabinet that contained dozens of trays, drawers, doors, and receptacles from which the doctor administered unending misery.

After seeing one of these cabinets in a restored frontier town, I began considering a similar layout to contain the many small items necessary for tying flies. The requirements for a good fly-tying station were established, and it then became obvious that reference books and bulk fly-tying materials could just as well be stored in the same cabinet. Over a two-year period, the scope of the undertaking ranged from suitcase proportions to a volume requisite for small farm hay storage.

Keeping in mind that I live in a modest house, the following is a list of the compromises made for a headquarters sufficient to hold what I considered to be the most necessary requirements:

1. a surface for tying flies and other work, at least 24'' wide
2. fly-tying tool storage within easy reach but off the work surface
3. material storage
4. reference bookshelf

5. bulk material storage
6. a place for fly rods
7. a place for fly boxes, extra lines, and reel spools
8. storage for tools used to repair and maintain rods and reels

All of the above had to be contained in a cabinet not more than about four feet wide, and because of some marital compromises, had to look somewhat better than an oversized orange crate. The other half of the marital deal included a closure of some kind to hide the mess of tying flies in a hurry.

The plans as shown may or may not fulfill your individual needs, but they can be modified to suit your tackle. For example, if you have more than about three dozen books, you can add another bookshelf. If you require more rod storage, and want a place for fishing jackets, the side wings can be enlarged.

An option that I seriously considered was to design the desk-top storage around a couple of small-parts cabinets that are available in several sizes. These cabinets would have offered more storage than the eight, relatively large drawers that I used. Should you decide to use these cabinets, you can improve the looks of the plastic drawers by sawing or grinding off the plastic pulls, and adding thin mahogany veneer to the drawer fronts.

List your particular needs carefully, and allow for future accumulations before deciding on your own headquarters.

You will find in some instances that the construction steps appear to be out of order. For example, the rod case stiles are ripped during the time that the case members are cut out. The reason for doing this is that when you set the saw for the top rabbet, you can also use this setting for the rod case rabbets.

In other cases you will not find specific dimensions, because the piece being cut is dependent upon work that was done previously. An example of this is the plough for the small drawer guides. The guides were installed during case construction and the drawer components are cut much later. It's easier to simply hold a drawer side in its respective position for marking, make the plough, install the side, and mark the next one relative to the one in position. This same procedure is used later in the book when building the Hook Chest.

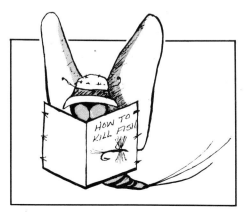

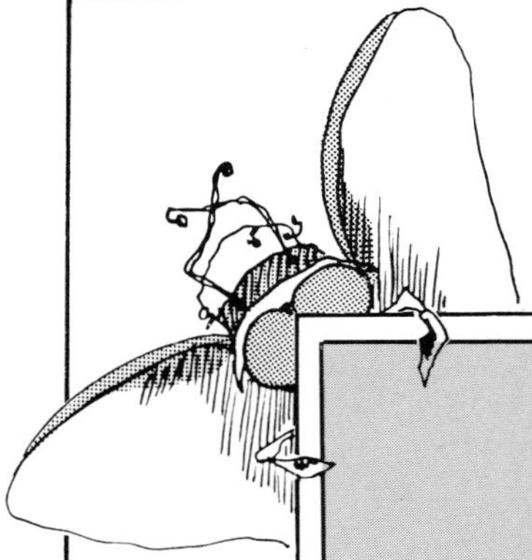

Material List

1 pc.	¾'' x 4' x 8'	mahogany plywood
1 pc.	¼'' x 4' x 8'	mahogany plywood
1 pc.	¾'' x 4' x 4'	high-density particle board
18 b.f.		½'' fir or pine
*50 b.f.		¾'' mahogany
12 s.f.		¼'' plywood or masonite
8 s.f.		⅛'' plywood or masonite
1 each		30'' piano hinge
4 each		large drawer pulls
10 each		small drawer pulls
6 each		door pulls
6 each		catches
7 pair		hinges
Misc.		scrap pine for base supports, drawer guides (approx. 10 b.f.), glue, nails, finishing material

* Note: When ordering mahogany lumber, the longest piece must be 5'9''. Widest pieces are approximately 10'' for raised panels.

Building the

Fishing Headquarters

As you read through these plans and instructions, you will encounter some construction methods that may seem a bit unconventional if you are an experienced cabinetmaker. Using occasional nails to fasten members together has always been looked upon as a vulgar furniture building procedure, and if this practice offends your building expertise, you may want to rely strictly on fine glue joints. However, exotic joints and complicated milling procedures have been purposely avoided so that construction can be accomplished by those with minimum shop facilities—mainly a table saw and jointer. The raised panel doors are cut on the table saw and sanded on a table sander. If you have access to a shaper with the proper cutters, it will save considerable work in the door construction.

One of the problems encountered when working with a complete cutting list of exact component sizes is that very slight errors in cutting are compounded as you progress. For this reason, only the main component dimensions are given, and the remaining pieces (face frame, etc.) are carefully marked in their respective positions, then cut to length. In some cases, you may want to make a trial piece from scrap wood to check the fit before cutting the final piece.

Building the Case

Begin construction by cutting the sides, top and base as shown in Drawings #1 and #2, then cut the ¾'' wide x ¼'' deep dadoes also shown in Drawing #2.

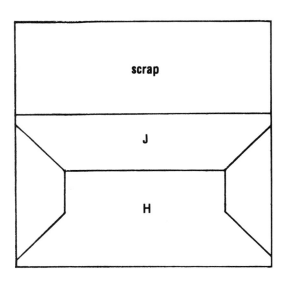

¾''x4'x4' H.D. particle board

A & B = sides
C = desk top 29'' L. x 17¾'' W.
D = lid 26'' L. x 14'' W.
E = desk shelf 29'' L. x 8¾'' W.
F = library bottom 29'' L. x 10½'' W.
G = bookshelf 29'' L. x 8¾'' W.
H = base
J = top

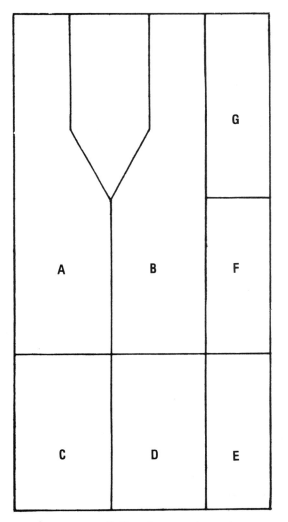

¾''x4'x8' mahogany plywood

DRAWING #1: General layout—see text and drawing #2 for actual dimensions

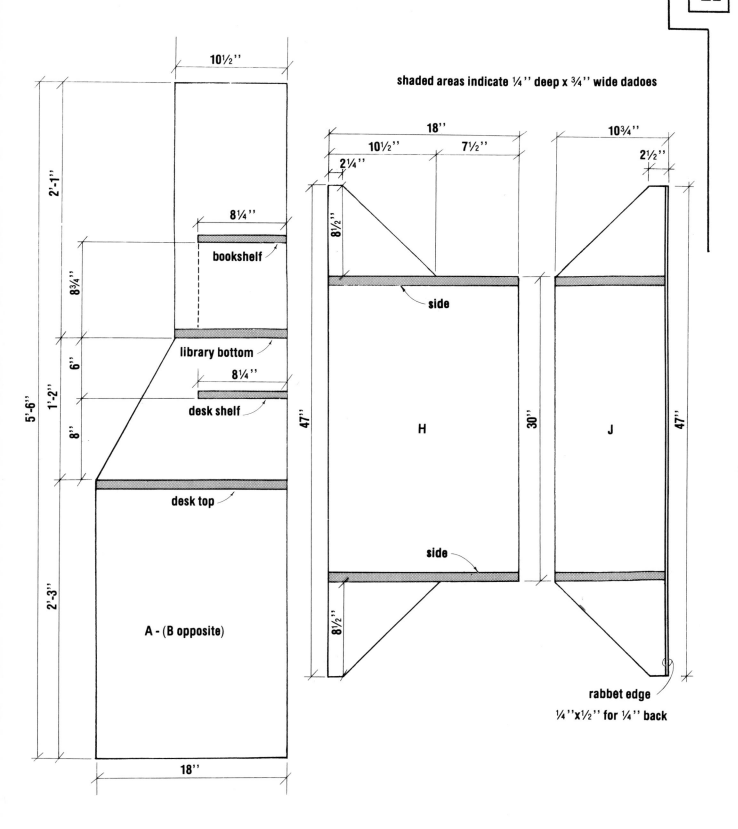

shaded areas indicate ¼'' deep x ¾'' wide dadoes

10½''

8¼''

bookshelf

library bottom

8¼''

desk shelf

desk top

2'-1''

8¾''

6''

8''

5'-6''

1'-2''

2'-3''

A - (B opposite)

18''

18''

10½''   7½''

2¼''

8½''

side

47''

side

8½''

H

30''

10¾''

2½''

J

47''

rabbet edge

¼''x½'' for ¼'' back

**DRAWING #2: dimensions and locations of various cabinet
components**

Cut the desk top 29'' L. x 17¾'' W., the book shelf 29'' L. x 8¾'' W., the desk shelf 29'' L. x 8¾'' W., the library bottom 29'' L. x 10½'' W., and the desk lid approximately 26'' L. x 14'' W. Apply a ¼'' x ¾'' solid wood strip to one long side of all pieces except the library bottom (F).

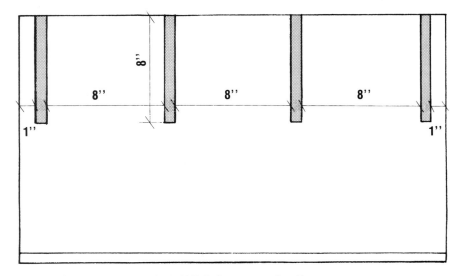

DRAWING #3: Desk top has ¾''x¼'' dadoes to receive dividers. Use this same layout to dado bottom of desk shelf.

Dado the desk top and shelf as shown in Drawing #3 and Photo A. Cut one similar dado, centered, in the bottom of the bookshelf and the top of the library bottom to receive the bookshelf support. Using the piano hinge as a gauge, cut a rabbet in the desk top and lid as shown in Drawing #4.

PHOTO A: Stopped dado in desk top and shelf. [Desk shelf shown in background.]

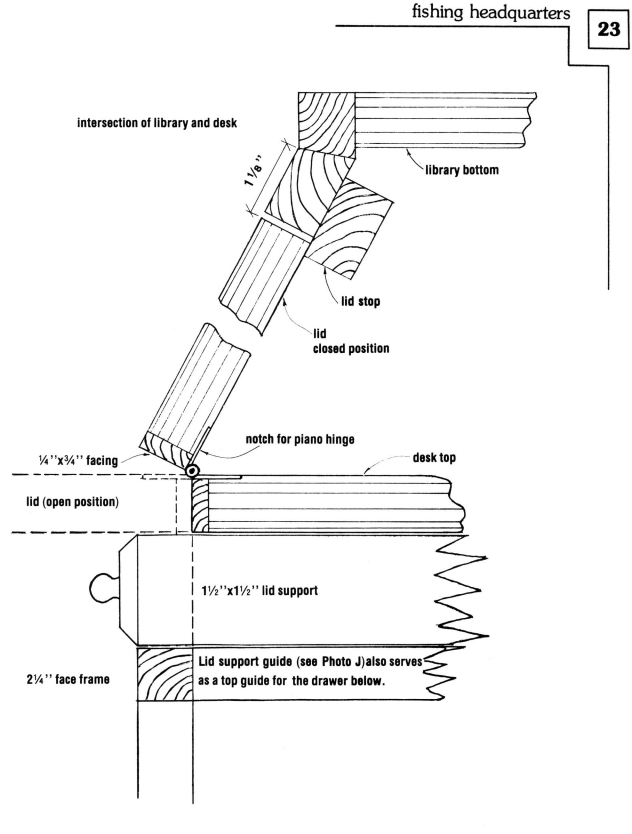

intersection of library and desk

1⅛"

library bottom

lid stop

lid
closed position

notch for piano hinge

¼"x¾" facing

desk top

lid (open position)

1½"x1½" lid support

2¼" face frame

Lid support guide (see Photo J) also serves
as a top guide for the drawer below.

DRAWING #4
After desk lid is trimmed for length, it is temporarily installed
and marked 1⅛" from the intersection. Cut lid at this point,
re-install, then cut beveled face frame rail to fit.

Rip two pieces of solid mahogany approximately 3 ⅛ '' W. x 5'9'' L. for the rod case sides. (The bevel cut shown in Drawing #5 will be cut later.) Now rabbet these two pieces, and the top piece J, ¼'' x ½'' as shown in Drawings #2 and #5.

Rabbet sides and top ¼''x½'' for back.

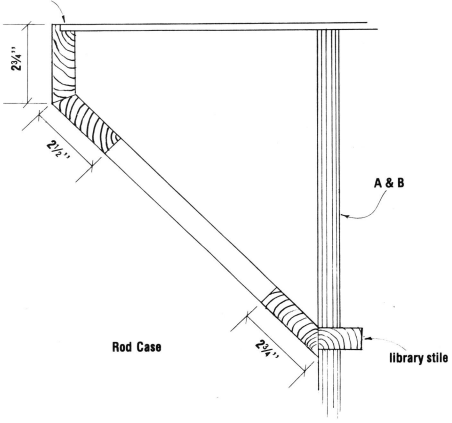

2¾''

2½''

Rod Case

2¾''

A & B

library stile

DRAWING #5: Using the cabinet base as a guide, lay out the bevel angles with a bevel square, and rip the bevels on the table saw. Use small pieces of scrap pine for trial cuts before cutting stiles.

Rip some ¾'' scrap pine to 2¼'' for the base supports, and cut to length using the bottom outside dimensions as shown in Photo B (the base is shown inverted). Glue and nail the supports to the underside of the bottom.

PHOTO B: Base supports nailed and glued to bottom of base.

Cut the 4 desk dividers, and 1 bookshelf support to 8½'' L. x 8½'' W. from solid ¾'' mahogany. Set the jointer for a ¼'' cut and make the stopped cut shown in Drawing #6 on both ends of the dividers, bookshelf support, bookshelf, and desk shelf. Photo A also shows a typical stopped dado.

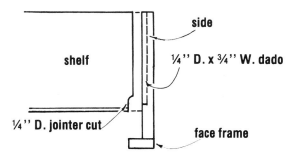

shelf

side

¼'' D. x ¾'' W. dado

¼'' D. jointer cut

face frame

Stopped Dadoes

DRAWING #6: This is a typical dado that is stopped short of the full shelf width. A ¼''x¾'' jointer cut allows the shelf to butt into the side member. Use this joint on the desk dividers, bookshelf support, bookshelf and desk shelf.

Cut the 16 drawer guides from scrap pine to ¼'' x ⁷⁄₁₆'' x 8¼'' L. Carefully lay out the guide positions on each of the 4 dividers. This layout is made so that the guides are centered on each of the 4 drawers (see Photo C). Glue and nail the guides.

PHOTO C: Glue and nail drawer guides to desk dividers. There is a guide centered on each of the four e-qual-depth drawers.

Begin case assembly by gluing the desk dividers into the dadoes cut in the desk top and desk shelf. Check for square, and allow the glue to set up.

Using glue and nails, assemble the sides, top and bottom pieces. Now slide the desk divider assembly into the proper side dadoes, glue, and nail. Do the same for the library bottom, bookshelf, and bookshelf support. Check the case for square (Photo D), and allow glue to set up. You may want to take a temporary diagonal brace to the back to hold the cabinet square.

This completes the assembly of the main case components with the exception of the ¼'' back.

PHOTO D: Main case components assembled.

Adding the Face Frame

All of the solid mahogany used for the remaining components should be ripped 1/8'' wider than the dimension given. After ripping, joint 1/16'' from each edge for the final desired width. The one exception is that the beveled stiles for the rod cases are jointed on one edge then cut on a bevel to the finished width. Joint and cut these stiles per the layout in Drawing #5, using 5'9'' as a finished length. Finished widths for the remaining stiles and rails are as follows: top rail - 3'' W. x approximately 48'' L., bottom rail - 3'' x approximately 88'' L., library and desk side stiles - 1⅞'' x approximately 72'', center stiles - 1¼'' x approximately 42'', top desk rail - 2¼'' x approximately 30'', 2 drawer rails - 1¼'' x 30''. The two rails at the intersection of the library and desk lid are shown in Drawing #4.

Notice that the final length of all stiles and rails is determined as they are put into position on the cabinet.

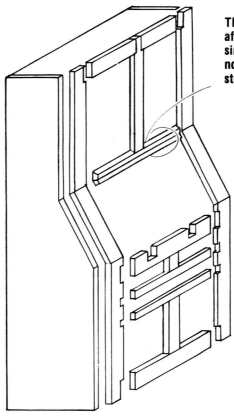

These two rails are installed after the desk lid is installed to simplify its fitting. They are not notched into the side stiles.

General Face Frame Layout

(rod cases not shown)

Notching the stiles, i.e., vertical members (see Photo E) to receive the rails produces an interesting joint that is simple to make and provides great strength when glued and blind nailed as shown in Photo F. The notches in the stiles are marked using their respective rails for the layout. Allow 3'' for the rail spacing to accommodate the top drawers, and 4½'' for the single large drawer. Apply the beveled stiles as shown in Drawing #5 using glue and fine brads.

The cabinet at this stage is shown in Photo G.

PHOTO E: Notching stiles on the table saw to receive rails.

PHOTO F: Glue and blind-nail face frame joints.

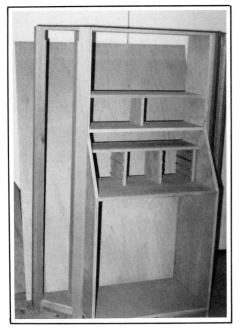

PHOTO G: Cabinet ready for ¼'' back. Measure inside of rabbets for overall back size.

PHOTO H: Desk lid—cut and fit width, then mark lid at a point 1-1/8'' from intersection, remove and cut.

The ¼'' back can be cut to fit, then glued and nailed in place. Apply the pre-notched stiles to the cabinet front with glue and clamps. If nails are necessary, use them where they will be covered with the top and bottom moldings if possible. Now mark the bottom and desk rails for length by placing one end into a notch and marking the other end with a sharp knife. Cut the rails, then glue and blind nail as shown in Photo F.

Before adding the beveled rails at the intersection of the desk lid and library bottom, you will want to fit the desk lid. Cut the desk lid 1/8'' less than the distance between the stiles. Temporarily attach the piano hinge with 3 screws in each leaf and check the gap on each side of the closed lid. See Photo H. Trim the lid if necessary. Now mark the lid 1⅛'' from the intersection as shown in Drawing #4. Remove and cut. The two beveled rails can now be cut and installed. To simplify installation, these rails are not notched into the stiles. Add the lid stop, center stile and upper rails, and glue these pieces in place as shown in Photo I.

PHOTO I: Beveled rails, lid support, and upper face frame in place.

PHOTO J: Lid support guide (shown inverted). Finished inside dimension is 1½'' x 1½''.

Glue and nail the lid support guides together as shown in Photo J. Glue and nail support guides in place. Notice that the bottoms of these troughs act as an upper drawer guide for the two drawers below.

Carefully sand the entire face frame, paying particular attention to the joints to avoid cross grain scratches.

The top and base moldings are cut to the shape shown in Drawing #7. Glue and clamp the top molding pieces together and allow to dry. Cut moldings to length and apply with glue and fine finish nails.

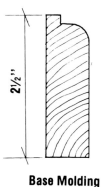

2½''

Base Molding

2¼''

2¼''

Crown Molding

DRAWING #7: both crown and base molding are made from ¾'' lumber. Quarter round and cove cuts are made with a table saw molding head, router or shaper.

Drawers

There are two kinds of drawer construction involved. The small drawers (inside the desk area) are guided by means of the ¼'' x ⁷⁄₁₆'' strips previously fastened to the desk dividers. The drawer sides are ploughed to receive the guides.

The base cabinet drawers are center-guided by a single rail that is ½'' wider than the face frame rail into which it abuts. This extra ½'' projects above the face frame and fits into a notch cut into the back of the drawer. Base cabinet drawer bottoms fit into ¼'' x ¼'' grooves that are ½'' above the bottom edge of the sides, front and back.

Rip the small drawer fronts, back and sides to 2'' wide, then joint 1/16'' from each edge. The resulting 1⅞'' width will provide the necessary clearance between drawers. The length of the drawer front is determined by measuring between the desk dividers, and subtracting 1/16'' for clearance. Subtract an additional inch from this length for the length of the drawer backs. Cut the sides 8'' long.

The drawer fronts are beveled as shown in Drawing #8 and Photo K, then sanded.

PHOTO K: Beveling drawer front on the table saw.

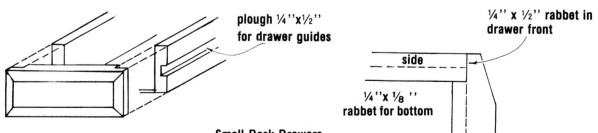

plough ¼''x½'' for drawer guides

¼'' x ½'' rabbet in drawer front

side

¼''x ⅛'' rabbet for bottom

Small Desk Drawers

DRAWING #8: Use ½'' pine for the sides and back of the small drawers, and ¾'' mahogany for the finished front that is rabbeted ½'' x ¼'' to receive sides. Plough for drawer guide is laid out by holding the drawer side against the guides on the desk dividers and marking with a sharp pencil.

Now set the table saw for a ⅛" x ¼" rabbet cut, and rabbet the bottom edge of the sides, front and back to receive the 1/8" bottom. Cut a ¼" x ½" rabbet in each end of the drawer fronts. The drawer sides can now be ploughed ¼" x ½" for the previously installed guides. This requires a careful layout and you will find that it is easiest to plough a side piece, install it on a guide, and then measure for the next one. Remember to allow approximately 1/8" between the drawers for clearance.

Temporarily assemble the 4 drawer pieces and measure for the bottoms. Cut the bottoms, and using glue and small nails, assemble the drawers. Photo L shows a small drawer ready for the bottom.

PHOTO L: Small drawer ready for 1/8" bottom.

The base cabinet drawers are built slightly different because they are larger and require more strength. If a means of producing dovetail joints is available, it would provide even greater strength and traditional styling. The method shown is relatively simple to build, however, and results in a satisfactory drawer.

Rip and joint the components as previously described, allowing approximately 1/8'' for vertical clearance. Rabbeted joints ¼'' x ½'' are used at all corners and are shown in Drawing #9. Measure the opening width and subtract 1/16'' as before, then subtract an additional ½'' for the false front and back. Cut the sides to 17'' long, and cut the ¼'' x ½'' rabbet at each end. Cut a ¼'' x ¼'' groove ½'' from the bottom edge of all 4 pieces to receive the bottom. Cut the ¼'' bottom to fit inside the grooves, then glue and nail the front, back, sides, and bottom together. Check for square. The finished drawer front is added using 1'' screws installed from the inside.

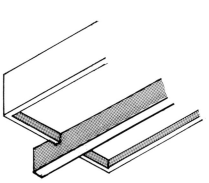

Underside of Base Cabinet Drawer

A simple wooden center drawer guide is used for the base cabinet drawers. Cut the guide ½'' wider than the face frame rail and 18'' long. Install in the center of the drawer opening with the top of the guide ½'' above the rail. A notch, ½'' x ¾'', is cut into the center of the bottom of the drawer back, to slide on the guide. Wax the guides with paraffin.

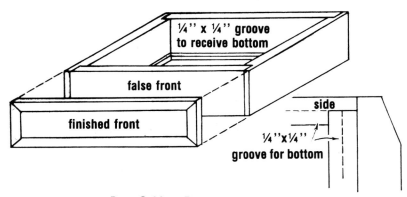

Base Cabinet Drawers

DRAWING #9: Base cabinet drawers have a finished front applied with screws through the false front from the inside.

Doors

The raised panel doors shown are constructed in a manner entirely different from conventional methods. The construction does not involve the use of a shaper or any special milling machine, and produces an attractive traditional door. Doweled joints have also been widely used and are highly recommended. When storage racks and tool racks are added, they actually strengthen the door and permit the use of the more simple spline joint.

Begin by measuring the door openings, and cutting the vertical and horizontal members slightly longer than needed. Rip and joint the pieces to the following finished widths: Rod case: verticals 1¾'', bottom 4½'', top 2½'', intermediates 2¼''; base cabinet and upper desk doors: verticals 1⅞'', top 2½'', bottom 3¼''.

Determine the exact height of each door opening and cut the vertical pieces accordingly. (Do not allow any clearance at this time, so the door can be trimmed to size after assembly). The length of each horizontal piece is determined by subtracting the width of the two verticals from the opening size. Now cut all of the horizontal (top, bottom, and intermediate) pieces to length. The dimensions for the rod case door panels, starting at the bottom, are approximately 15'', 14'', 11'' and 9''. You may have to adjust your spacing slightly to arrive at your final total length.

Set the table saw for a ¼'' wide x ⁷/₁₆ '' deep plough cut, ¼'' from the rip fence. Placing the **face** of each piece against the fence, cut the grooves that will receive the raised panels and splines.

Cut the ¼'' splines from 7/8'' wide plywood strips. Assemble the 4 pieces of a typical door using the splines but no glue. Now add ¾'' to the inside dimensions, and cut the center panels. Using a piece of scrap wood, cut the bevel shown in Drawing #10. Now sand

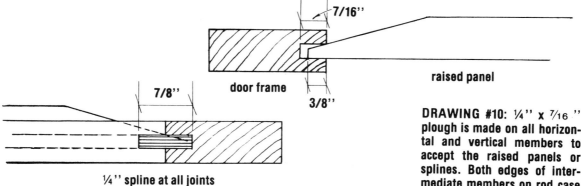

7/16''

door frame

3/8''

raised panel

7/8''

¼'' spline at all joints

DRAWING #10: ¼'' x ⁷/₁₆ '' plough is made on all horizontal and vertical members to accept the raised panels or splines. Both edges of intermediate members on rod case doors are ploughed.

the scrap to remove saw marks, and slide it into one of the grooves. The idea is to have the raised panel go exactly 3/8'' into the groove without forcing the fit or having a gap. Once the setting for a good snug fit is made, bevel and sand all of the raised panels.

Assemble doors on a flat surface covered with newspaper (see Photo M). Glue all splines and joints but

PHOTO M: Door components ready for assembly.

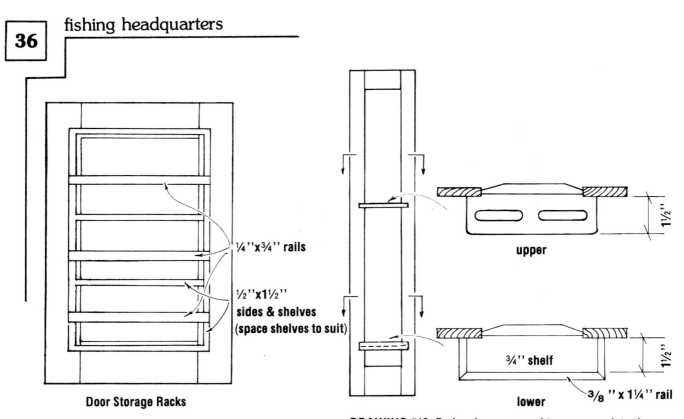

Door Storage Racks

¼''x¾'' rails

½''x1½''
sides & shelves
(space shelves to suit)

upper

1½''

¾'' shelf

1½''

³⁄₈ '' x 1¼'' rail

lower

DRAWING #12: Rod racks are spaced to accommodate the shortest rod sections to be stored. Use 2'' brass screws to fasten rack shelves to door frame.

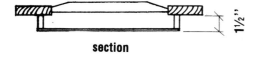

1½''

section

DRAWING #11: Door storage rack is a simple frame made from ½''x1½'' stock fastened to door frame with 2'' screws. Lay out shelves and rails to allow materials to be stored and removed easily.

don't glue the panels in place. The panel must be free to expand and contract slightly with changes in humidity and a rigid joint will eventually result in a cracked panel. After the glue has dried, trim doors to fit openings with approximately 1/16'' clearance all around, then sand. Hang the doors, using three 2½'' brass butts on each rod case, and two 2'' brass butts on the others.

The lid supports are 1½'' square by 18'' long, and can be glued up from 2 pieces of ¾'' stock. Sand to fit and bevel front edges.

Drawings #11 and #12 show a method for suggested storage and rod racks. For fly-tying tools, two strips of wood ½'' x 1½'' can be drilled to suit your needs. Add

PHOTO N: Tool racks inside
upper door.

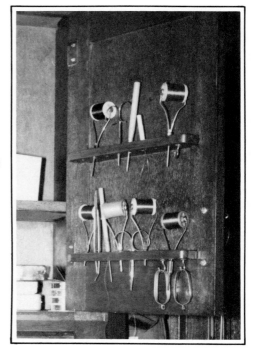

a few small brass cup hooks to the underside of the
strips for hackle pliers, etc. See Photo N.

Photo O shows suggested door storage racks which
can also be used on the base cabinet doors.

PHOTO O: Material storage
rack.

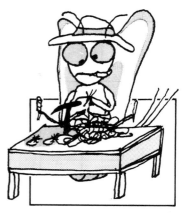

Finishing the Headquarters

There are several opinions as to the best way to finish furniture, especially if it is built from an open grain wood like oak or mahogany. I shall take you through the process that I use, but suggest that you contact local finishers to see their finished product, and to ask for their suggested methods.

Remove all of the door hinges and catches prior to the final sanding and finishing.

Sanding is the most critical step toward a fine finish. I start with 80 grit paper to remove scratches and machine marks. All lumber that is surfaced was run through a planer and planers leave machine marks or waves in the finished surface. If the planer feed was set too fast these marks will be very pronounced. Nevertheless, they are always present, even in plywood, and have to be removed.

I use progressively finer paper until all scratches and marks are gone. The final sanding is done with 220 grit paper followed by a thorough vacuuming.

Mix a small amount of paste wood filler and stain together and apply it to a piece of scrap mahogany with a brush. After about ten minutes remove the excess filler by rubbing across the grain with a piece of burlap. The idea is to leave only the amount of filler required to fill the porous surface and no more. Let the scrap wood dry overnight. The next day, use steel wool to rub the surface down. Now apply a light coat of furniture lacquer. The end result will show what your cabinet will look like.

If I am not satisfied with the color on the scraps, I adjust the color of the stain/filler mix by adding darker or lighter stain. Once I have the right combination, I apply it to the cabinet doing one complete area at a time so that I can rub it down without leaving lap marks.

I steel wool the surface after 24 hours and vacuum it off.

In the cleanest, dust-free shop that I can prepare, I begin to apply the lacquer in thin coats, rubbing each coat down with steel wool when dry. Three to five coats are required.

Re-hang the doors and re-install the catches. Carefully mark and drill the holes for the door and drawer pulls and attach them.

Now all you need is about half the neighborhood to help you move the cabinet from the shop to its final resting place.

When tying flies, I use a light-colored desk pad to provide a light background and protect the desk top. Add an adjustable lamp that can be removed to allow you to close the desk lid.

"a well tied fly"

Izaak's Desk

Introduction

Izaak's Desk was first introduced in an article published in **Fly Fishing The West** in December 1980. At that time, finished units, kits, and plans were available for sale. After a few months I turned the desk over to the Orvis Company of Manchester, Vt., and they sold the finished units through their catalog and retail outlets for a year or so. The desk design was modified, changed to oak, and built by a wood-working company in the East. The project is relatively labor-intensive, so it was expensive and enjoyed a rather narrow market.

This is my own patented design, but it was interesting to find that during the patent search, the attorneys found six other similar designs dating back to 1874!

When used as a lap desk with a clamp vise, use the

upper left drawer for storing items that are used in all tying sessions (vise, bobbins, hackle pliers, etc.). Place these tools on the work surface or in the tool racks and remove the drawer. Open the bottom drawer slightly and clamp the vise to the top with the lower stem inside the drawer. Reverse for left-hand operation.

The spool console, light-colored Lo-glare Formica top, raised drawer fronts and brass hardware have all been combined to provide the ultimate in convenience and traditional styling.

I have chosen to present the Izaak's Desk plans in this book just as I had them copyrighted in 1980.

Izaak's Desk
Building Instructions

The tying bench built from these instructions is a quality, functional, work table designed by fly tiers. Construction, as shown, should not be attempted by the inexperienced, or by those not thoroughly familiar with the proper use of tools. However, using the basic overall dimensions and concepts, you may modify the construction to suit your ability and shop facilities. These tables are usually built from fir, tamarack and fir plywood, but you may want to substitute other woods.

A low-glare plastic laminate such as Formica is recommended for the work surface, since it provides a hard stain-resistant top. For those who prefer wood, a durable varnish, such as one used for gym floors, should be applied.

Begin by carefully reading through the instructions and checking the material list.

1. Cut the top and sides from ½'' plywood to the dimensions shown. The divider is cut from ¾'' ply or solid stock.

2. Cut the ¼'' back and bottom, then glue and nail the ½'' nailer strip flush with the rear edge and centered on the top of the bottom.

3. Dado the underside of the top for the sides and divider (Drawing #2).

4. Rabbet the rear edge of the top ¼'' x ¼'' to within 3'' of each end. Rabbet the sides ¼'' x ¼'' along the back and bottom. Note, the left and right sides have opposite cuts. Dado ¼'' x ½'' for drawer guides per Drawing #3.

5. Assemble top, divider, sides, back and bottom with brads and glue. Apply plastic laminate top with contact cement and trim edges.

6. Glue up 3 pieces fir ¾'' x 1¾'' x 22¾'' to form a 1¾'' x 2¼'' x 22¾'' console. Drill 1½'' holes per Drawing #2. Rip console at 41° as shown in Drawing #6, then joint all surfaces and sand.

7. Cut console base as shown in Drawing #6. Caution —this is a large cut so you may want to make the base from 1 pc. ¼'' x ¾'' and 1 pc. ¼'' x 2''. Drill 3/16'' holes per Drawing #2.

8. Cut tool holders and sides then drill 3/8'' and pilot holes as shown in Drawing #2 and #4.

9. Assemble with glue and brass screws, and epoxy brazing rod pins in place.

10. Add 9/16'' x 3/8'' or 1/2'' x 3/8'' top trim. Note— if plastic laminate is used, trim must be 9/16''. Glue and nail.

11. Cut all drawer parts per Drawing #5 and assemble with glue and nails. Carefully locate drawer guides to line up with dadoes in sides and divider. Nail and glue.

Sand all parts to remove scratches and tool marks. Stain, varnish and add drawer pulls. Wax guides for smooth operation.

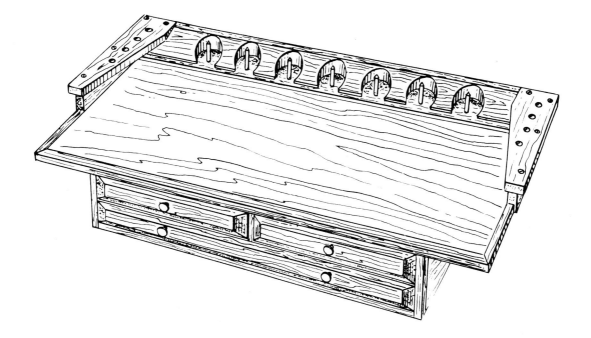

Material List

Quantity	Description	Size	Remarks
1	Top (plywood)	½''x11½''x22¾''	
2	Sides (plywood)	½''x11½''x4¾''	
1	Divider (plywood)	¾''x11¼''x2⅛''	
1	Back (plywood)	¼''x3¾''x16¼''	
1	Bottom (plywood)	¼''x11¼''x16¼''	
1	Nailer (solid)	½''x½''x15¾''	
2	Tool racks (solid)	½''x2¼''x8½''	
2	Tool supports (solid)	½''x2⅛''x8''	
1	Console (solid)	1¾''x2¼''x22¾''	(Glue up 3 pc. ¾)
1	Console base (solid)	¾''x2½''x22¾''	
1	Top trim (solid)	½''x³⁄₈''x36''	(Cut into 3 pc.)
1	Face trim (solid)	¼''x¼''x12''	(Cut into 3 pc.)
4	Drawer sides (solid)	½''x1¾''x10½''	
2	Drawer backs (solid)	½''x1¾'''6⁷⁄₁₆''	
2	Drawer fronts (solid)	¾''x1¾''x7¹⁵⁄₁₆''	
2	Drawer bottoms (ply)	⅛''x6¹⁵⁄₁₆''x10¼''	(or Masonite)
2	Drawer sides (solid)	½''x2¼''x10½''	
1	Drawer back (solid)	½''x2¼''x14¹¹⁄₁₆''	
1	Drawer front (solid)	¾''x2¼''x16³⁄₁₆''	
1	Drawer bottom (ply)	⅛''x15³⁄₁₆''x10¼''	(or Masonite)
7	Pins (brass)	³⁄₁₆''x1½''	
3	Pulls (brass)	½'' diameter	
16	Brass screws	#6x1'' r.h.	
1	Drawer guide	¼''x⁷⁄₁₆''x72''	(Cut into 6 pc.)
1	Optional top surface		
	(Plastic laminate)		
	Brads, glue, epoxy, sandpaper		

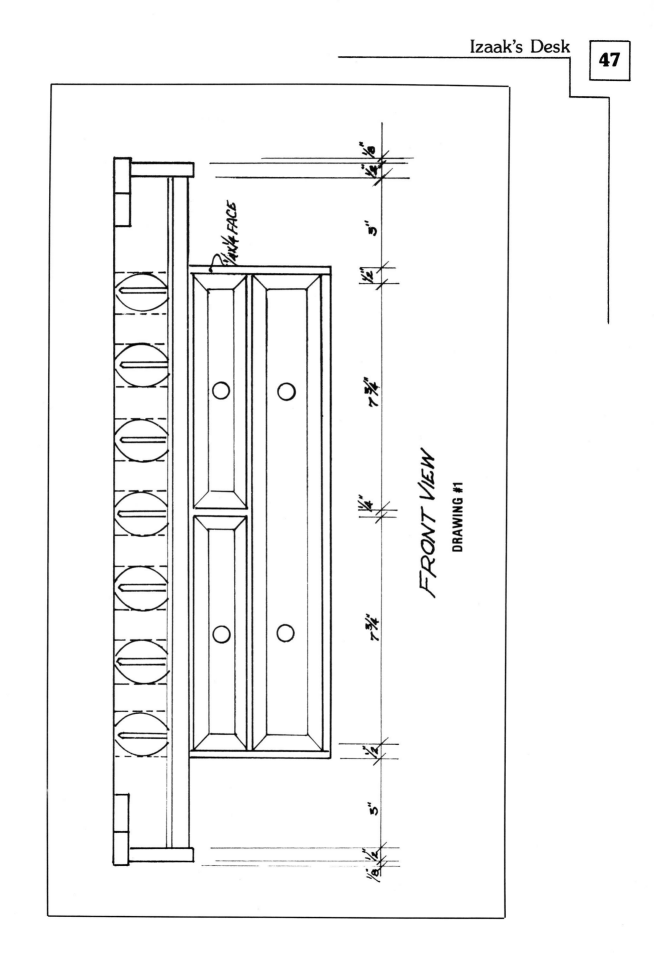

FRONT VIEW
DRAWING #1

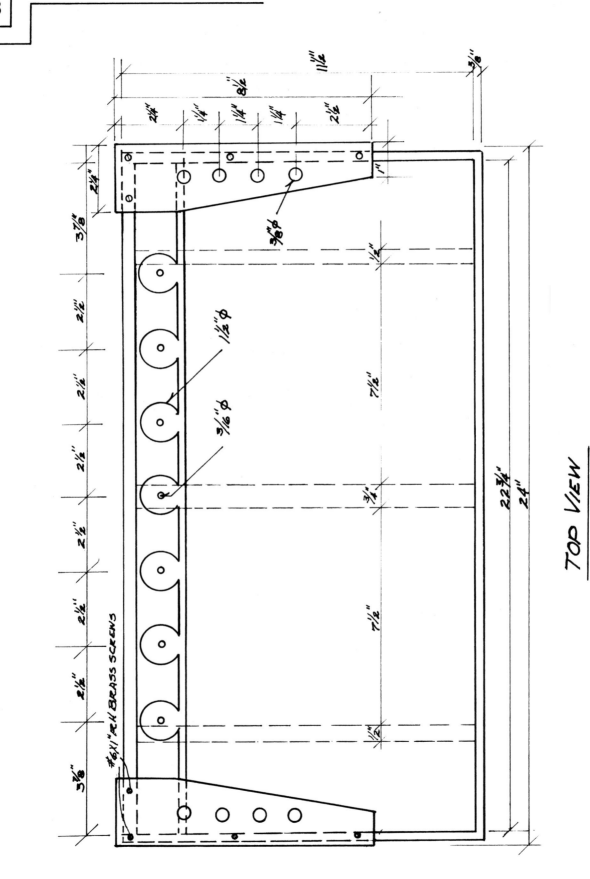

TOP VIEW

DRAWING #2

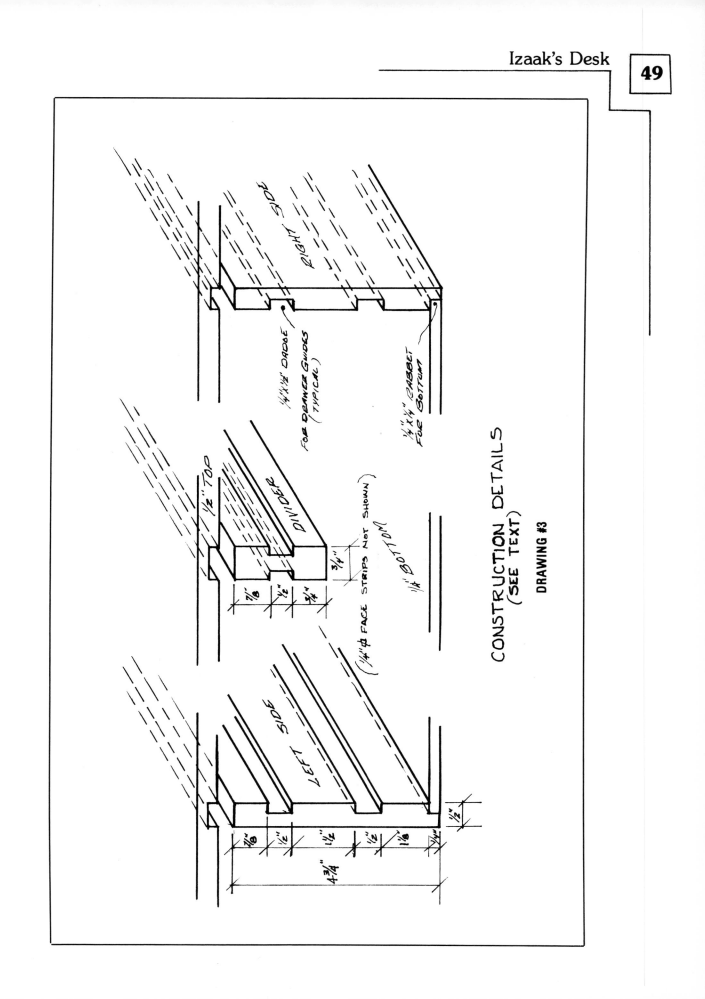

RIGHT SIDE

¼"×½" DADOE
FOR DRAWER GUIDES
(TYPICAL)

¼"×¼" RABBET
FOR BOTTOM

½" TOP

DIVIDER

(¼"ø FACE STRIPS NOT SHOWN)

¾"

⅛" ½" ¾"

¼" BOTTOM

LEFT SIDE

⅛" ½" 1½" ½" 1⅛" ¼"

4¾"

½"

CONSTRUCTION DETAILS
(SEE TEXT)

DRAWING #3

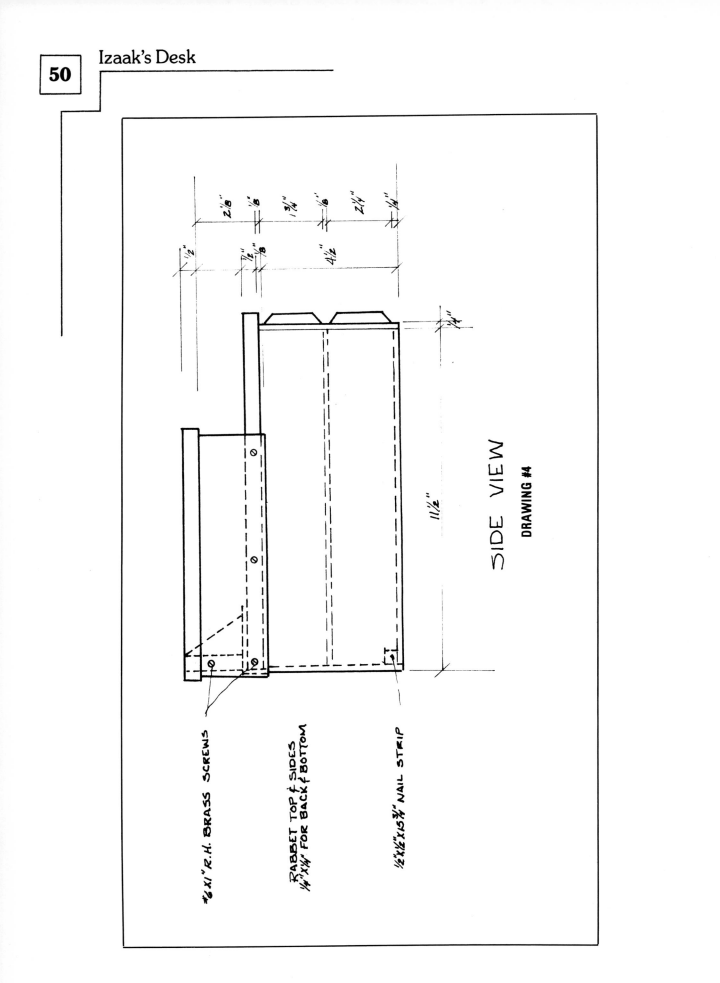

SIDE VIEW

DRAWING #4

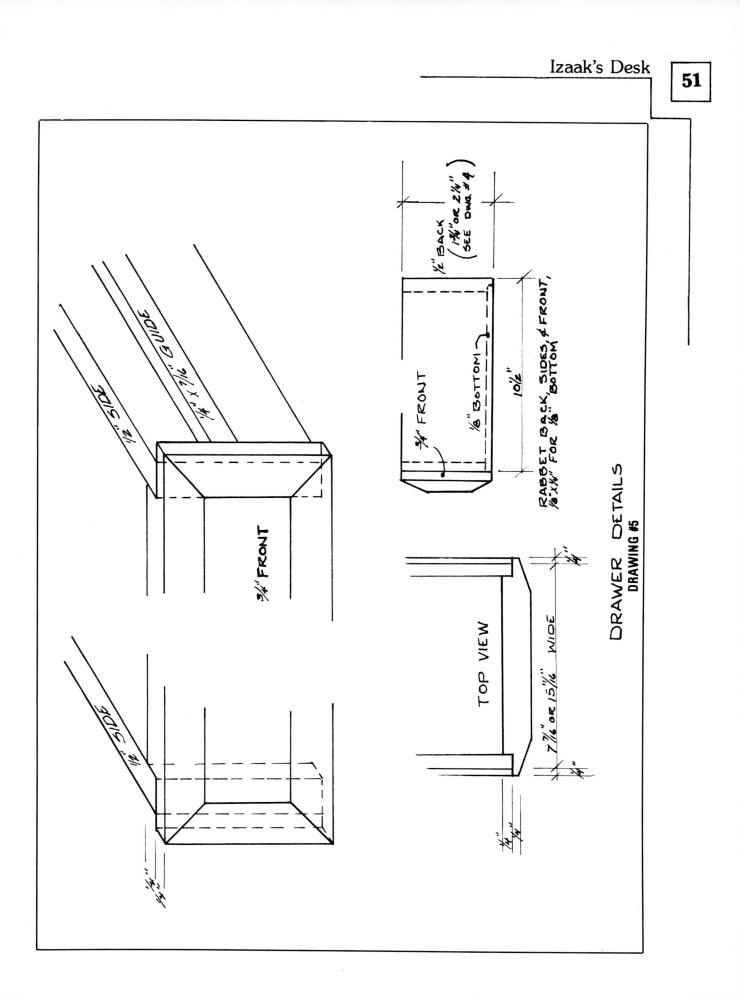

DRAWER DETAILS
DRAWING #5

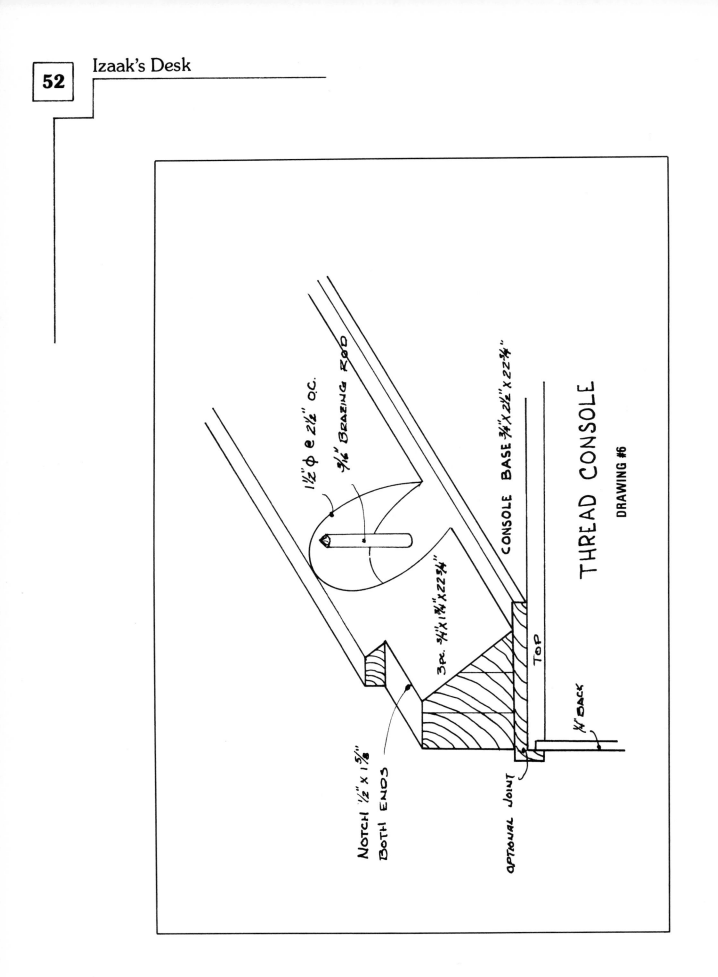

NOTCH ½" X 1⅝" BOTH ENDS

OPTIONAL JOINT

1½" φ @ 2½" O.C.

⁵⁄₁₆" BRAZING ROD

3 PC. ¾" X 1¾" X 22¾"

CONSOLE BASE ¾" X 2½" X 22¾"

TOP

¼" BACK

THREAD CONSOLE
DRAWING #6

A Fishing Box

Introduction

There is something mystical about a well-constructed wooden box with brass trim. Stained and varnished hardwood, when battered and gouged with time, assumes a character that is flattering and often even preferable to its original polish.

While others may hurry to the workshop to repair a dent or re-stain a scratch, I have always accepted the consequences of use as reminders of the forays upon which the abuse was inflicted.

I built a true tackle box back in the 1950s and it has served faithfully for 30 odd years. The box is in semi-retirement now since the hardware and plugs that it contains are of little use to a fly-fishing convert. Occasionally, a trip to eastern Montana in pursuit of walleyes will add a few more lines to its weathered countenance; but its real importance to me lies in its stereoscopic memories that have covered many thousands of miles.

The Fishing Box (''tackle box'' is not the proper term) is presented with the lines and dimensions that I happened to use. I believe that my scientific approach to the size question consisted of measuring the scrap wood in my shop at the times of inspiration and inception. However, some importance should be placed on the dimensions of what will eventually go into the box. It should also be fairly stable and reasonably portable.

Material List

½'' oak plywood or solid lumber:
    top, bottom and ends . . . . approx. 5 s.f.

¼'' oak plywood:
    front and back . . . . .approx. 3 s.f.

½'' oak lumber (other scrap may be used)
    band, ledge, fly box . . . . .approx. 2 b.f.

⅛ '' Masonite or Marlite:
    fly box lid and bottom . . . . .approx. 1 s.f.

Miscellaneous:
½'' elastic
1 pr. brass butterfly hinges
8 brass chest corners
2 brass chest hasps
1 brass lid support or chain
1 brass chest handle
½'' brass escutcheon pins (optional)
stain, filler, brads, glue, varnish

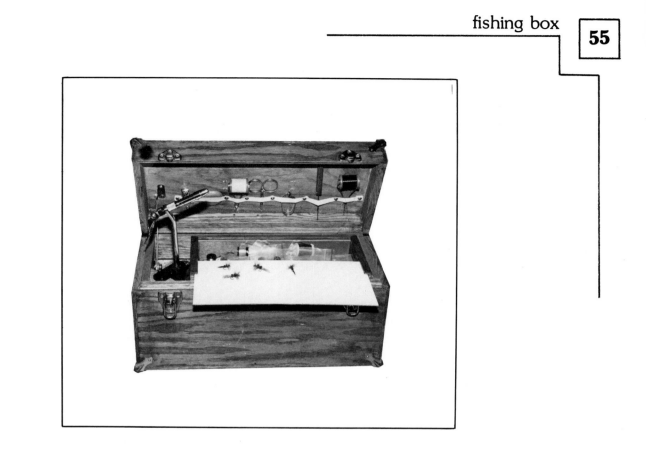

The Fishing Box

Here is a project that I built one winter just because I happened to think of a few items I needed to take along when fishing with my car-top boat. The original idea was to have something in which to carry shear pins and a few small tools for my trolling motor; but as you will see from the following list, the box now goes on all fishing trips.

A fairly extensive fly-tying kit has become the most used part of the box. The kit only measures about 5½'' wide x 11½'' long x 2'' high, but by using small ziplock bags, you can store dozens of fly-tying ingredients in a very small space. The idea is to carry a wide variety but small quantities of material. It is unlikely that you would ever tie more than a half dozen of any one pattern before returning to your ''mother lode'' of materials.

The list may change tomorrow, but as of today here's what I'm carrying in the box in addition to the fly-tying kit.

Two fly reels and two extra spools

4-way screwdriver

Small crescent wrench

Small pliers

Regular pliers

Fillet knife

Knife sharpener

Shear pins and keys

Motor manual

Fly line conditioner

Reel repair tools and oil

Wader repair kit

Extra tippet material

Matches

Rod guides

Tip tops

Ferrule cement

Small flashlight, extra batteries

Camera and film

First-aid kit

Fly-tying kit utilizes zip-lock bags.

And I still have room for a couple of extra fly boxes.

Notice that the box has no compartments or dividers. If you have specific space requirements, you might consider partitions. If so, I suggest that you make the partitions removable.

The overall dimensions that I used are: 16'' long x 7¼'' wide x 8¼'' high. The top, bottom and ends are ½'' oak plywood; and the front and back are ¼'' oak plywood.

The overall dimensions of each piece are:

Top & bottom: ½'' x 7¼'' wide x 16'' long

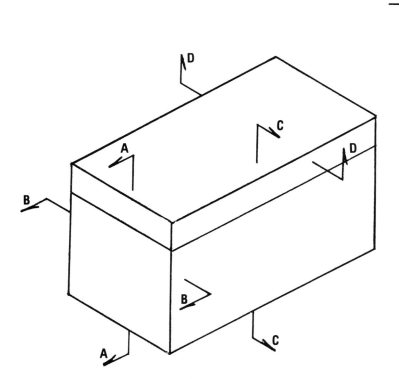

Fishing Box Construction Details

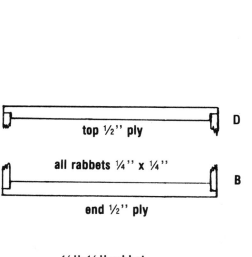

top ½'' ply

all rabbets ¼'' x ¼''

end ½'' ply

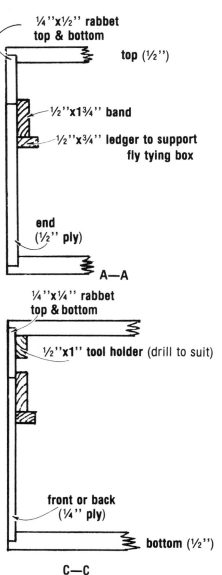

¼''x½'' rabbet
top & bottom

top (½'')

½''x1¾'' band

½''x¾'' ledger to support
fly tying box

end
(½'' ply)

A—A

¼''x¼'' rabbet
top & bottom

½''x1'' tool holder (drill to suit)

front or back
(¼'' ply)

bottom (½'')

C—C

Ends: ½'' x 7¼'' wide x 7¾'' high

Front & back: ¼'' x 15½'' long x 7¾'' high

After the rabbets in the top, bottom and ends are cut as shown, the box is assembled using glue and ¾'' brads.

When the glue has dried, sand all of the surfaces and ease the corners slightly. The box is now cut to separate the top from the bottom at a distance 2'' down from the top. At this stage, you can add ½'' brass escutcheon pins along all edges. These pins add a nice touch but are only for decoration, and if used, they must be added after the sanding.

Add a ½'' x 1¾'' wooden band around the inside of the top edge of the bottom. This band projects ¼'' above the bottom to provide a rabbet for the top to close against. Glue and nail a ½'' x ¾'' ledger under this band to support the fly-tying box. Now add a ½'' thick x 1¾'' triangle to the left front on which to clamp the vise.

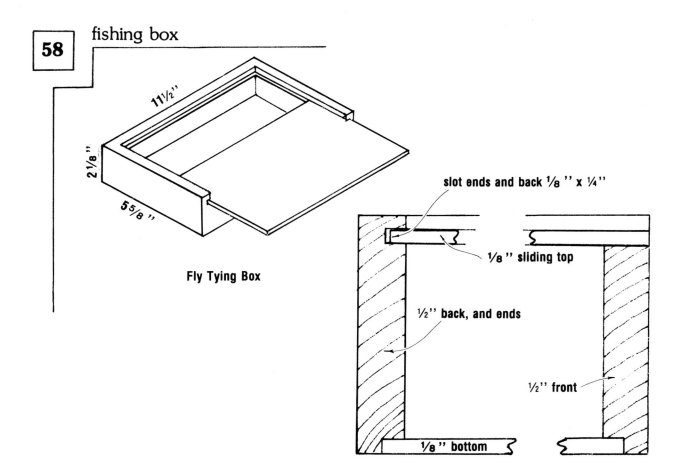

Fly Tying Box

slot ends and back ⅛" x ¼"

⅛" sliding top

½" back, and ends

½" front

⅛" bottom

Fly-tying tools are held in place inside the lid by means of a ½" x 1" oak strip and a length of ½" wide elastic fastened to the top with tacks or staples. Drill the oak strip at the back of the lid as required for your bobbins, scissors, etc.

The fly-tying box measures 11½" long, 5 5/8" wide and 2 ⅛" deep. The front, back and ends are ½" pine and the bottom and sliding top are 1/8" Masonite. Masonite is readily available, but if you can find the kind with baked-on white enamel, it will make a better fly-tying background.

Carefully align the butterfly hinges before drilling for the screws. Notice that even though the back is made of ¼" plywood, the screws extend into the ½" x 1¾" band at the box bottom and the ½" x 1" tool holder in the lid. This is also true for the two hasps on the front of the box. A brass lid support or length of chain is mounted inside the left-hand side of the box to hold the lid in an upright position when opened. Install the eight brass corner protectors and the handle.

Before finishing the box, remove all the hardware. Stain and fill the oak after a thorough, overall sanding. The box will, hopefully, be exposed to the elements for extended periods so the final finish has to be durable. Use a good spar varnish and apply according to manufacturer's specifications.

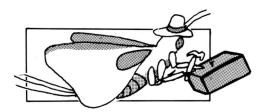

Part II

Scrap Wood

Projects

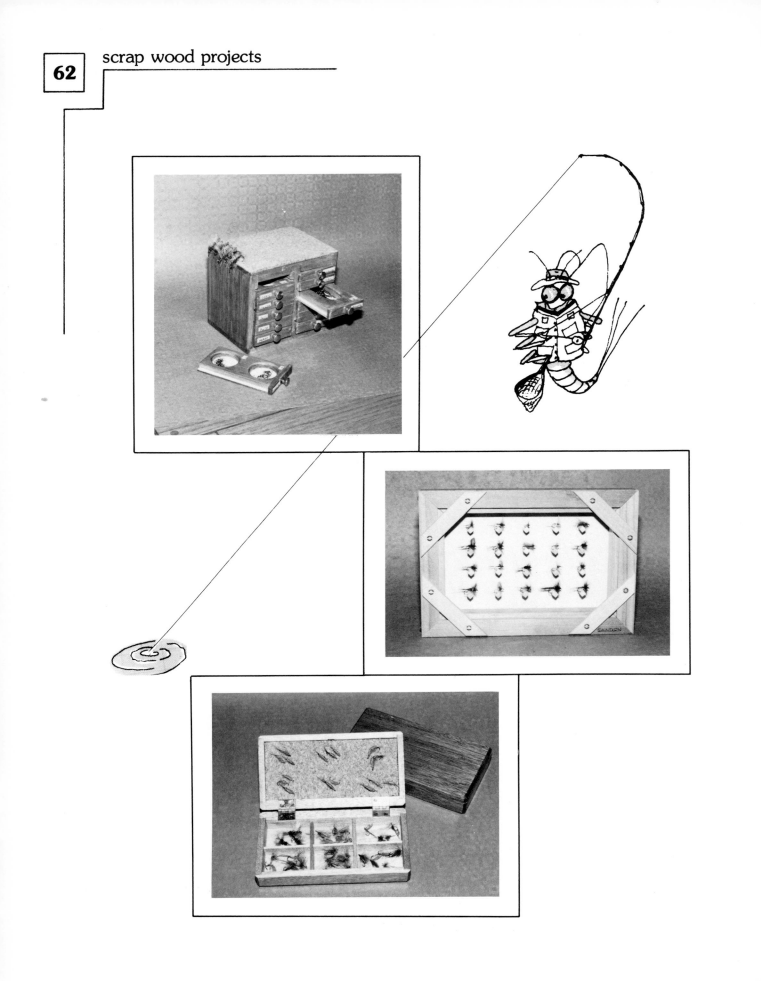

Fishing Headquarters
Features

FISHING HEADQUAR-TERS—A beautiful piece of traditional furniture designed to store and organize fishing gear as well as provide a functional work area.

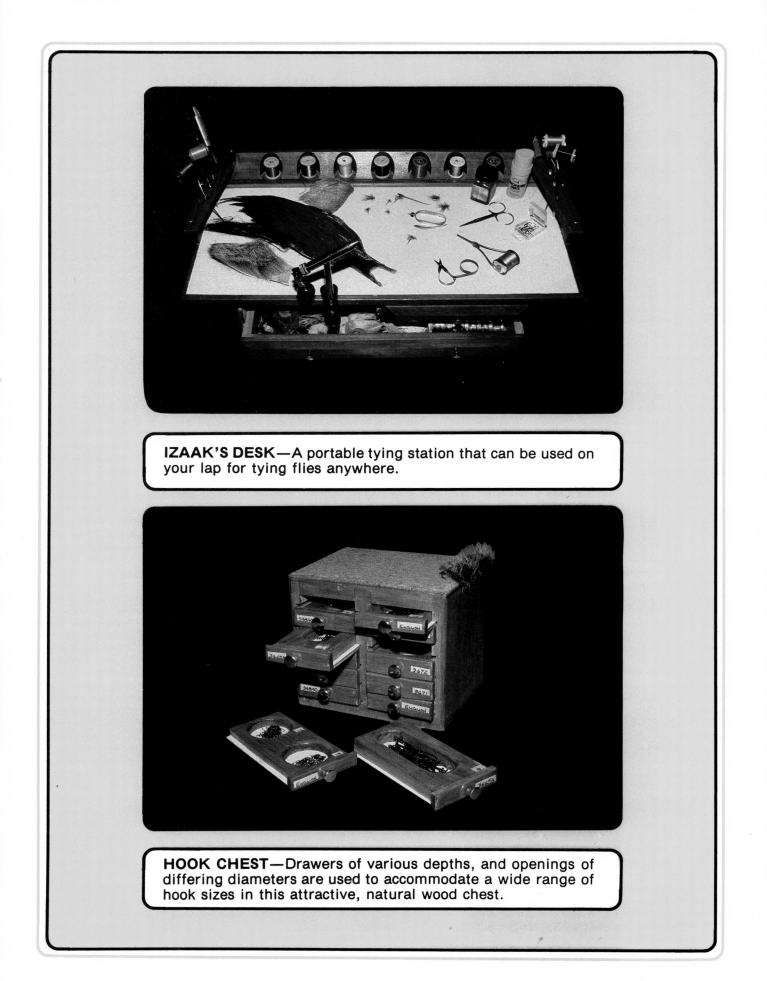

IZAAK'S DESK—A portable tying station that can be used on your lap for tying flies anywhere.

HOOK CHEST—Drawers of various depths, and openings of differing diameters are used to accommodate a wide range of hook sizes in this attractive, natural wood chest.

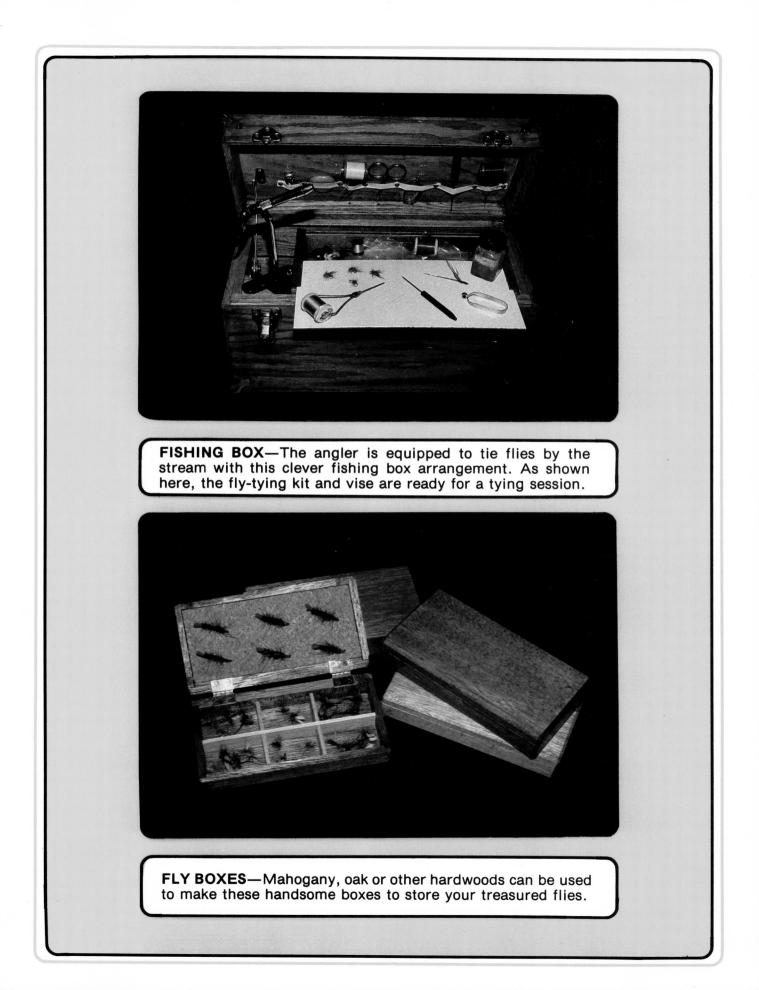

FISHING BOX—The angler is equipped to tie flies by the stream with this clever fishing box arrangement. As shown here, the fly-tying kit and vise are ready for a tying session.

FLY BOXES—Mahogany, oak or other hardwoods can be used to make these handsome boxes to store your treasured flies.

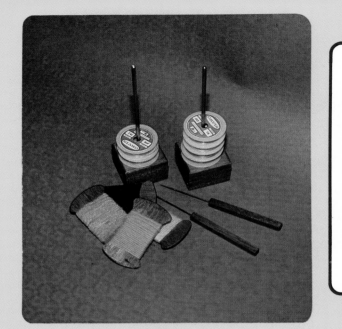

BODKINS, SPIN-DLES, AND YARD CARDS—Here are three simple desk accessories that are made from scrap wood that will add a nice touch to your fly tying and leader building.

FLY DISPLAY—Flies are tiny works of art that can be mounted and framed to make an attractive display.

ROD-WINDING DEVICE—This carefully designed instrument simplifies the work of installing or rewinding rod guides by dispensing the winding thread from fly-tying bobbins.

Scrap Wood Projects

Introduction

I f you are like most builders, you probably hate to throw anything away, especially small pieces of expensive hardwood. The following items are all usable in various angling inducements, but should be viewed as just a beginning toward creating other imaginative possibilities from scrap wood.

We are now at the juncture where harsh practicality starts to fade and artistry begins to emerge. This is a pleasant borderland that requires less discipline and more creativity.

This is the land where bodkins are carefully made of carved and rubbed hardwood with piano wire points ground to surgical sharpness. This is where you unwind chenille from stamped cardboard and rewind it onto thin mahogany pieces that captivate old-time thoughts.

This is your personal chapter, intended as a nucleus for projects that you can manipulate in your hands or hang on the wall.

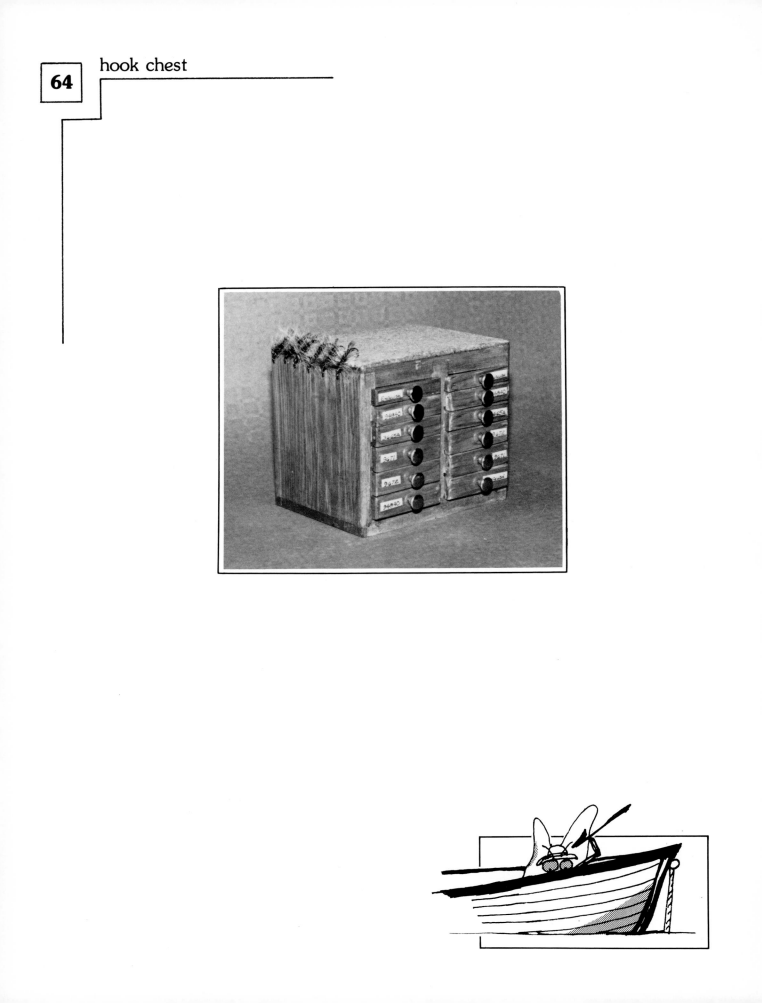

Hook Chest

Introduction

There is a certain brand of hooks that, in my opinion, are the finest you can buy. The problem is that the rest of the world evidently does not agree, so they are tough to find. I have always been partial to the odd sizes like 15 or 13 in dry fly quality, and not too many brands offer them. Occasionally I would come across a box or two in a shop and it took self-control to keep from breaking the glass to get my hands on them. The shop owners immediately knew I would have bought them at almost any cost as they silently cussed themselves for having the price displayed.

On a Missouri River fishing trip, I stopped at the Montana Fly Goods Company in Helena just because I had never been there. After I had the up-to-date scoop on the river conditions and red hot patterns, the conversation turned to fishing gear. When I mentioned my favorite brand X hooks, owner Doug O'Looney's face looked as blank as my financial statement. He told me that he had bought out the inventory of an unsuccessful shop, and that there were a few boxes of those hooks included, but he hadn't bothered to bring them to the store. Pity immediately clouded his face as he watched me froth and stammer.

"If you want them, I'll bring them in tomorrow," he said. Just as I started to regain some composure, he added, "They won't cost you anything." I still haven't fully recovered.

Not long after that trip, I started thinking about some kind of a hook storage facility in which I could proudly store my new windfall. The result is the following hook chest.

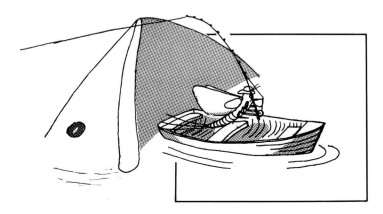

Building the Hook Chest

If your normal fly tying doesn't require more than a couple dozen hook sizes, you should build one of these. You might want to experiment with the size and number of drawers to suit the hook models and sizes you use. The chest shown will hold 3,000 to 4,000 hooks.

Small drawers would normally require dozens of tiny pieces that you would have to assemble with tweezers, and they probably wouldn't be very sturdy. The solution to the problem is to make the drawers from one piece of drilled wood, then add a bottom that will also serve as the drawer guide.

The drawers in this chest vary from 3/8'' to 5/8'' thick which will store a wide range of hook sizes. For example, the ½'' deep drawer with a 1½'' hole in it can easily hold 200 size 12 standard hooks, or several hundred of the smaller sizes. Some of the drawers have two holes while the larger sizes of long-shank hooks require one elongated compartment made by drilling two holes and sawing out the connecting wood. The drawers shown measure 2¼'' wide x 4½'' long, and the 1/8'' bottom is 2¾'' wide x 4½'' long.

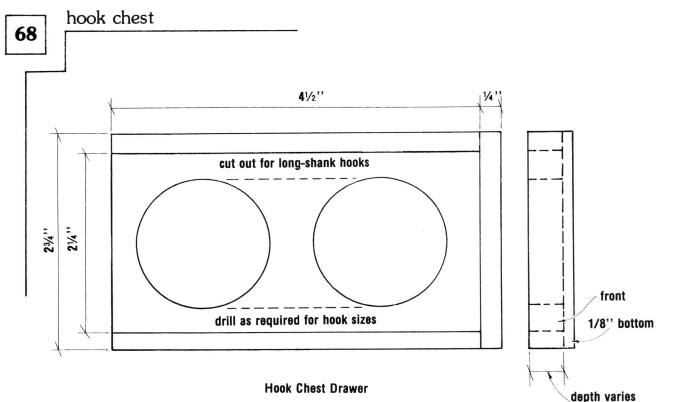

4½" ¼"

cut out for long-shank hooks

2¾" 2¼"

drill as required for hook sizes

front

1/8" bottom

depth varies
from 3/8" to 5/8"

Hook Chest Drawer

Now drill the holes for your hooks. A drill press with a hole saw works best, but a portable drill will work if you clamp the drawer to a solid surface to prevent splitting. Round the top edge of each hole with a ¼" round-over router bit or by hand with a half-round, fine rasp.

There should be just enough space between the drawers to allow them to slide. This snug fit prevents the hooks from slipping between the drawers if the

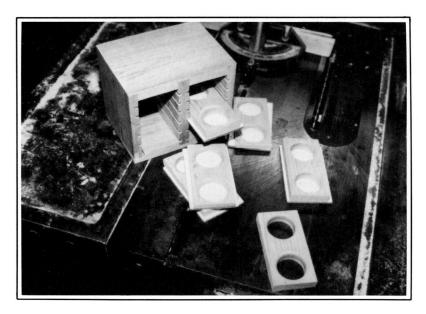

chest is tilted. I won't even give you a layout for the guide slots because if it's off by a pencil mark to start with, the error compounds six times before you are through. Besides, there is an easier way.

Cut the top, bottom, and sides 4¾'' wide by about 7'' long to start. You can use ½'' to ¾'' thick material. The back is ¼'' plywood, so rabbet these pieces ¼'' x ¼'' on the back edge to receive it. The center divider is 4½'' wide because it butts into the back, and is cut to about 7'' long for now.

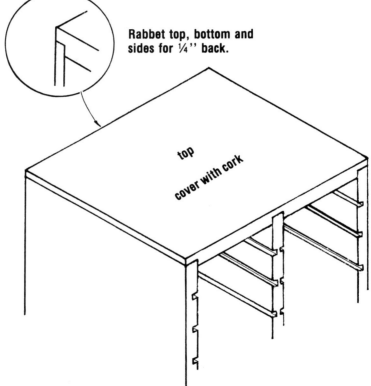

Rabbet top, bottom and sides for ¼'' back.

top

cover with cork

Hook Chest: Lay out groove spacing by using the actual drawers & bottoms.

Lay out the top piece so the sides and center can be notched into it. For example, if you are using ½'' material for the sides, top, and bottom, and ¾'' for the center divider, start at one end of the top and make a mark at ½'' then measure 2 5/16 '' for the first drawer. (This allows 1/16'' clearance.) Now mark for the ¾'' center divider, 2 5/16 '' for the second drawer, and ½'' for the second side. Cut the top to length at this point. Then lay out and cut the bottom the same way.

Set the table saw blade for a ¼'' deep cut and make the end rabbets and center dado in both pieces. Insert the sides and the divider into the rabbets and dado of the top piece, temporarily.

Hold the top drawer and bottom pieces in place against the underside of the top. Using a knife, mark the position of the 1/8'' bottom. Now using the same ¼'' saw setting, cut the groove to receive the drawer bottom. Repeat for all three pieces. Slide the first drawer into place, and put the second drawer in position so you can mark its grooves. This process is repeated until all six grooves are cut into the sides and center divider.

After the last grooves are cut, add ¼'' to the three pieces and cut them to length. This ¼'' goes into the rabbets and dado in the bottom. Slight adjustments for drawer clearance are made with a sander.

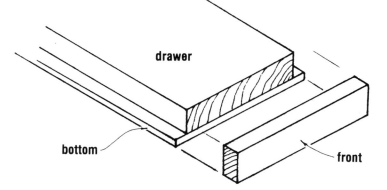

Glue the drawer to its bottom; add a ¼'' thick drawer front to each. Each front is 2¾'' wide and as high as is required to cover the drawer and its bottom.

After assembling the case with glue and nails, I added a 3/16'' cork top to my cabinet and rounded all of the corners. The cork provides a handy place to dry flies when tying.

Finish the cabinet with stain and varnish and make some paper labels to identify hook model numbers. Glue the labels to the drawer fronts. Other labels for identifying the hooks are glued onto the drawer by their respective holes.

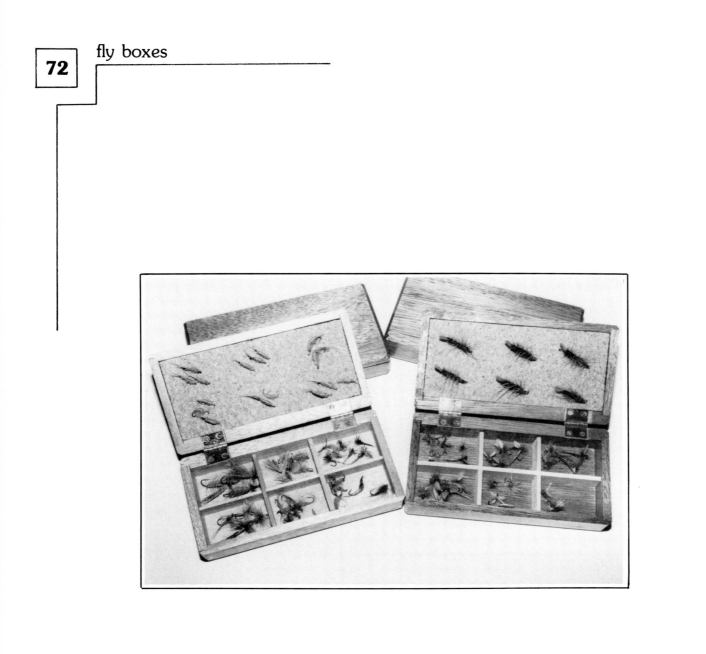

Presentation Fly Boxes

Introduction

This little project was an enigma. It was rewarding, yet absolutely frustrating. When the Orvis Company was marketing Izaak's Desk a few years ago, I asked them what they thought of the idea of an Executive Fly Box made of hardwood. They were mildly enthused and asked the usual questions about price and production, to which I responded in my most aggressive business voice: ''I dunno.''

As part of my research, I built two boxes and sent them to Orvis for their evaluation. They liked them.

In the meantime, I visited a company that builds beehives and all of the related frames and tiny inside things that go with them. I took three fly boxes with me. One was finished, one assembled and unfinished, and one unassembled.

''Yup, we can build um,'' they said after microscopically examining each piece.

''How much?'' I asked.

''I dunno,'' the man said. But he quickly assured me that after his partner returned from marketing hives in Afghanistan they would price out the whole package based on 1,000 units. I really wasn't too optimistic at that point.

To condense the rest of this story, the hive people gave me a price, and Orvis said: ''Let's try a few.'' The difference between the construction price of 1,000 labor-intensive boxes and the offer to ''try a few'' was enough to scare me off. Besides, I got work building a chicken coop for a neighbor—cash money.

Building the Fly Box

Round up at least enough material to build two or three fly boxes at a time. I recommend mahogany for ease of working and the rich, traditional, final finish.

Begin by cutting from 3/16'' plywood or solid stock, the top and bottom exactly 3½'' x 6½''. The sides and front are ripped to ¼'' x 1⅛'', and then cut to 6½'' and 3'' long, respectively. The back piece is 7/16'' x 1⅛'' x 6½''. Cut a ⅛'' x ¼'' rabbet on the ends of the front and back pieces.

At this point, make a trial assembly and be sure that the top and bottom are just slightly larger than the assembled front, back and sides.

Glue all six components together and let set overnight. When the glue has dried, sand all of the edges with coarse sandpaper on a flat surface. This sanding is to remove any irregularities and square up the edges.

The 1⅛'' width allows approximately 1/8'' for a saw cut when ripping the top from the bottom after the pieces are assembled. Rip the top from the bottom at a point 3/8'' from the top surface. At this time, or just prior to this cut, you can chamfer all of the corners. A router works best for this cut but you could use a block plane and sanding block. Sand all surfaces.

Cut the dividers from 1/8'' plywood or solid stock and notch to make six ''egg crate'' compartments. The photo below shows a box glued together and the nine components required to build another.

Fly Box components

The hinges are Model #CD 5302 made by the Stanley Company, and measure ¾''x1''.

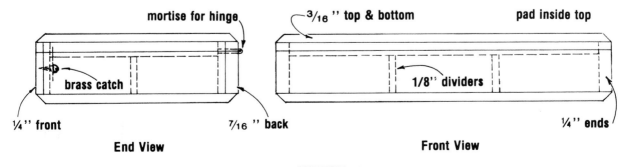

SKETCH #1

Mortise for the hinges and screw them into place. Next, cut the brass catch as shown in Sketch #2 and fasten in place with a #4x¼'' brass, round-head screw. When properly adjusted, the friction of this strip against the inside of the lid is sufficient to hold the box closed.

SKETCH #2   **A piece of thin brass fastened to the inside of the front holds the top closed.**

The pad inside the lid can be made of cork, foam, rubber, wool, or soft felt. Cut to size and set aside.

If you use mahogany, mix up some wood filler and dark mahogany wood stain. Rub this into the open grain and let it set up. Wipe down the excess filler-mix and, if necessary, repeat the process until the grain is filled. When you're satisfied with the stain, set the box aside for 24 hours.

There are many clear finishes on the market, but a spar varnish with an ultraviolet screen is one of the best. Thin the varnish with paint thinner and apply three or four coats, allowing each coat to dry thoroughly. A good finish is essential to prevent moisture absorption and subsequent warping.

Glue the pad inside the lid with Pliobond or a contact cement. Cut a small slot in the pad where the catch goes.

I don't fasten the dividers in place. I prefer to leave them loose to ease the cleaning of the box.

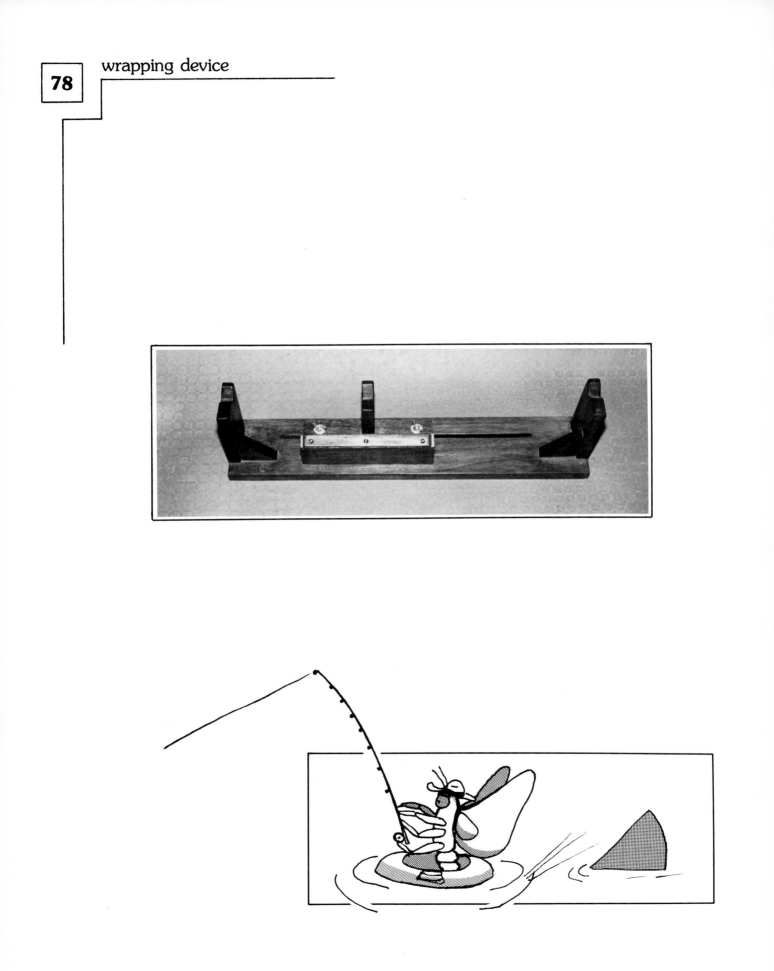

Rod Wrapping Device

Wrapping rod guides can be made easier with this simple little machine. The bobbins that you use for tying flies hold the thread with the proper tension. Tension is increased by wrapping the thread around the bobbin frame before threading. One or two turns usually provides the right resistance.

I built my wrapping device as an accessory for my fly-fishing headquarters, so scrap mahogany was used throughout.

The moveable center support allows wrapping guides close to the ends of rod sections, while the overall length of 24'' provides full support. Since there are no

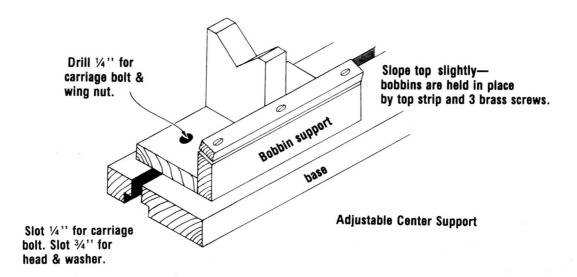

Drill ¼'' for carriage bolt & wing nut.

Slope top slightly—bobbins are held in place by top strip and 3 brass screws.

Bobbin support

base

Slot ¼'' for carriage bolt. Slot ¾'' for head & washer.

Adjustable Center Support

critical dimensions for this device, I suggest that you dig through the scrap bin and come up with your own. Generally, it can be about 6'' high, and 4'' or 5'' front to back for stability. A place to hold one bobbin is all you need for most rod winding, but if two color wraps are used, two places to hold bobbins (as shown) help speed up the winding.

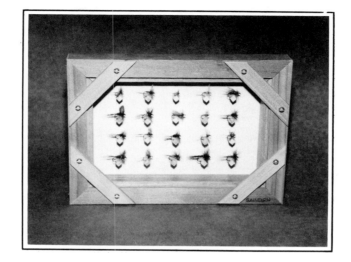

Fly Displays

Well-tied flies are tiny works of art. Even people who know nothing about fly fishing or proper fly proportions appreciate a nice display.

If you are making displays for gifts, or for sale, include colorful streamers and the old wet fly patterns. Most people are attracted to the tinsels, bright floss and variegated feathers from exotic birds.

Fly displays can be any size you want. I have made frames that measured 2''x 3'' for a single stonefly nymph, and a case for a hotel lobby display that contained over 160 patterns.

Fly displays can be any size.

All displays should have a glass front to protect the flies and keep dust out. The only critical dimensions are from the back to the glass (depth) and the spacing between the flies. Most flies will fit in a case with a 1 1/16 " depth, but check the ones you will be mounting first.

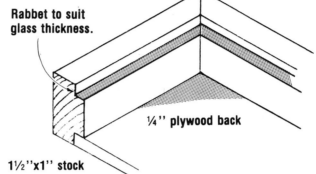

Rabbet to suit glass thickness.

¼" plywood back

1½"x1" stock

I use 1'' long x 5/16'' square pine pegs for mounting the flies, and drive them into ¼'' holes in the ¼'' plywood back panel, after carving the square corners off for about 3/8''. Lay out the flies on the back panel to get the most pleasing arrangement before drilling.

The frames can be built in several ways. The one shown is made from 1'' x 1½'' square-cut stock. The ¼'' back fits into a ¼'' rabbet cut into the frame members, and the front glass goes into a similar rabbet that is cut to accept the glass thickness. Use a ⅛'' x ¼'' cut for double-strength glass.

Carve corners of 5/16'' square pegs.

Assemble the frame by using two 1'' x #6 brass screws at each corner; and use brads to hold the back in place. The glass is held in place with a ⅛'' x ¾'' x 4'' strip of wood across each corner that is surface applied with two brass screws. These screws are easily removed for glass cleaning or to change fly patterns.

Another method, if you object to the corner pieces, is to cut a groove in the frame to accept the glass. This groove should be held back about ¼'' from the front of the frame, so make the frames about 1¾'' to 2'' deep.

As mentioned, peg spacing width depends on the patterns mounted. A rule of thumb to start with is that dry flies up to size 12 can have pegs spaced 1¼'' on center horizontally and 1'' vertically. Adjust the spacing for long streamers and high-winged drys. The spacing shown in the photo below leaves a lot of space between flies, so streamers could also have been mounted.

To insure that the flies are held securely, use soft pine for good hook penetration, then add a drop of instant glue to each one.

An important part of a fly display is the background color. White, blond, and badger hackles are difficult to see against a light background. You should group patterns according to their predominant shades, then select a contrasting background which can be adjusted with various wood stains.

Solid color backgrounds are made by applying poster board, cloth, burlap, wallpaper or vinyl to the plywood with the appropriate adhesive.

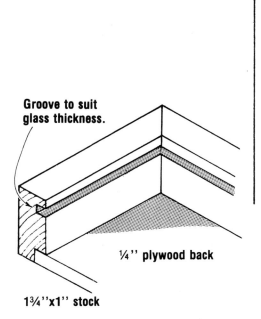

Groove to suit glass thickness.

¼'' plywood back

1¾''x1'' stock

Alternate Fly Display Frame

Space pegs as needed.

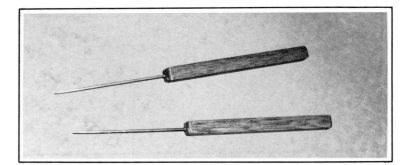

Bodkins

These are handy items that have many uses in fly tying. Rip some scrap hardwood to about 3/8'' square and cut it to approximately 4'' long. At a hobby shop, select a piece of piano wire that appears to be about the right diameter. I believe I used wire that is approximately .050'' in diameter, but I'm not sure, and it isn't critical anyway.

Piano wire is very hard and can ruin a pair of wire cutters. It's best to file a groove around the wire with a file, then break it. Cut a piece about 2'' long. Insert this length of wire into a drill chuck, then while the drill is running, hold the wire against a grinding wheel to sharpen it. When sharp, this becomes your drill bit.

Drill the wood handle at least 1'' deep. Now cut a piece of wire about 4'' long, coat 1'' of it with epoxy glue, then drive it into the drilled hole. When the glue has set up, grind the point using a long gradual taper.

Sand, stain, and finish the handle as desired.

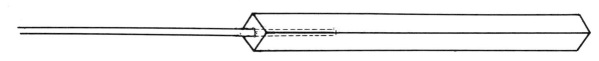

Bodkin Handle 3/8'' sq.

Yarn Cards

These cards just plain look nice. They don't hold yarn or chenille one bit better than the cardboard that it comes on. They are simply nice little desk accessories that don't really cost anything.

Rip some scrap to 1/8'' thick, or use 1/8'' plywood. Cut to the same outline as the cardboard holder or make up your own design. Sand, then finish as desired.

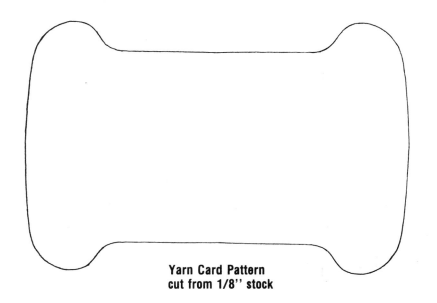

**Yarn Card Pattern
cut from 1/8'' stock**

Spindles

Building leaders is greatly simplified by using two spindles. Once you have the necessary number of leader spools of the right diameters, stack them in proper sequence on one of the spindles. As the spools are used, place them on the second spindle so they will remain in order. When you have completed a leader, invert the stack and start over.

You can make the wood bases as fancy as you wish. I chose mahogany to match the mahogany of my fishing headquarters, and made the bases 2¼'' square x 1½'' thick. The actual spindle is a piece of 3/16'' brazing rod about 8'' long.

The easiest way I have found to measure all of the pieces for making leaders is to lay an 18'' strip of masking tape across my work surface, and to mark it in 1'' segments. I lay the leader material against the tape and clip it to the proper length. This semi-permanent measuring device does not have to be handled, and can be disposed of after a work session.

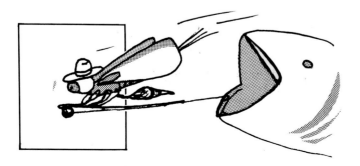

Keeping It All Together

A fishing headquarters is not the solution for every fisherman. Those who only fish occasionally and don't tie flies or have similar related hobbies need only to find a place for a couple of fishin' poles and a minimal amount of gear.

Simplistic fishing tackle reminds me of a time long ago when as kids in northeastern Montana we were the undisputed authorities on the subject. Selling beer bottles to buy a tin of assorted hooks at the local hardware store for five cents would put us in the fishing business for the entire season. Dad's carpenter tool box always contained chalk line; and sinkers in the form of nuts and bolts could be found just about anywhere.

Tonkin cane could not compare to those willows that grew along the muddy banks of the Milk River. Green, supple stocks were chosen carefully, and a good pole was carried over the shoulder to the river and back home for several days before it became dry and brittle. A new one was then carefully selected and cut with a "genuine barlow" jackknife. When brother Bobby and I were given rods and reels for Christmas one year, it was the holiday to end all holidays. I don't recall exactly what year it was, but if you research the longest winter ever recorded in Montana history, that's gotta be it. The ice must have gone off the river in late September that year.

Fine fishing equipment like we had could not be stored just any old place, so we would stand the rods in a corner of the kitchen with line and hooks still intact, ready for the next morning's fishing. When bits of worm or grasshopper were inadvertently left on the hooks, it was often necessary to spend a good deal of our time running to catch and release the house cat. Now every time I release a trout I'm thankful it doesn't hiss or have claws. Maternal discipline and a couple dead cats led us to the belief that there might be a better place for storing our fishing gear.

Tackle should be stored together and kept handy in case of an emergency. You never know when an overpowering impulse might lead you to water's edge; and precious time cannot be wasted looking through closets, nor can you take the chance of arriving at the scene without every essential piece of equipment.

During an overnight fishing trip on the Missouri, I forgot to take a flashlight and it practically ruined the trip. That particular stretch of the river is known for big browns and rainbows. Just after I finished supper they started **their** supper of freshly hatched caddis flies. The sun was going down as I waded into the feeding frenzy. After fighting and releasing a couple of nice trout it was completely dark; but the fish had just begun to gorge themselves. Huge trout slurped and splashed all around me as I stood in the middle of the river with hopelessly tangled leaders. After several trips to shore to turn on the car lights and replace snarled and broken leaders, I had had enough. The rest of the night was spent in the sleeping bag listening to ten-pound fish having a party.

The fishing box described earlier would allow you to keep a lot of your gear handy for your next outing, provided you remember to take the box. The logical solution to that potential problem is to have a place—a storage area—to keep all of your tackle together and away from the cat.

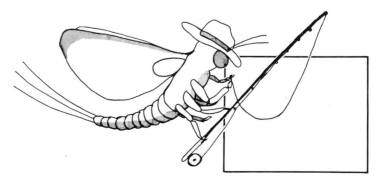

Simple Storage Cabinets

A locker like the metal military type works fine for tackle storage, or you can build one with proportions to suit your needs. Your garage or storeroom space will dictate whether the cabinet should be built for vertical or horizontal placement. The following are some suggestions and sketches for cabinet construction, layout, and size, but, as mentioned before, measure your gear and allow for future accumulations.

Expensive rods should be wiped down after each trip and stored in dry rod tubes to protect them. If you don't have store-bought tubes, they can be made from rigid plastic pipe.

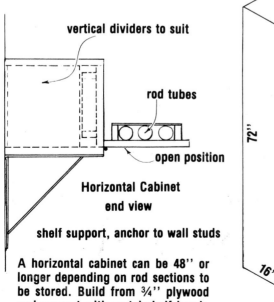

vertical dividers to suit

rod tubes

open position

Horizontal Cabinet
end view

shelf support, anchor to wall studs

A horizontal cabinet can be 48'' or longer depending on rod sections to be stored. Build from ¾'' plywood and support with metal shelf brackets. A cabinet of this type requires no floor space and can be mounted above a workbench. Use the top of the cabinet for a storage shelf.

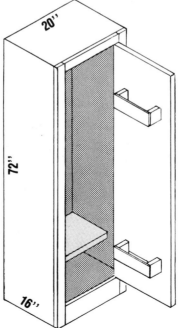

A vertical storage cabinet with some suggested dimensions, built from ¾'' plywood. Provides hooks or pegs for hanging vests, jackets, creels, nets, etc.

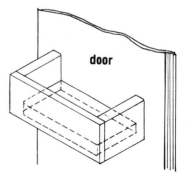

door

A simple rod rack is screwed in place with 2'' screws through the face of the door. The top rack is made the same as the lower rack, except for the bottom piece which supports the rods and tubes. Measure your rod tubes for rack dimensions.

Glossary

S ome of the terms used in this book may not be familiar to the occasional builder, and the following list is provided with a brief description of how the terms relate to these projects.

BEVEL—A cut made on the edge of a board that is not 90 degrees to the surfaces. The first step is to cross cut or rip a bevel on the table saw using scrap wood, to make a trial assembly. If the bevel is exposed or the saw cut is not smooth, use the jointer, set at the same angle, to finish the edge. Minor bevel angles are made with the jointer only, but use several passes rather than dangerously expose the jointer knives for a deep cut. The bevels for the raised panels and drawer fronts are slightly different and are shown on pages 31, 33 and 35.

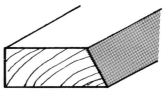

CHAMFER—A chamfer differs from a bevel in that it does not go from one surface to the opposite surface. The cut is usually 45 degrees and extends only part-way down the edge of a board. Cut with a jointer, hand plane, shaper or router.

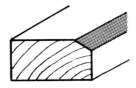

COVE—Cove cuts for moldings can be cut with a table saw molding head, if a shaper is not available; however, a table saw does not normally have enough speed for smooth cuts if a lot of material is removed. Use several small cuts to achieve the final shape. Router cove bits are available.

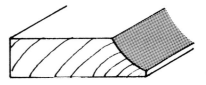

DADO—A groove that is cut in one member the same width as the thickness of the stock to be placed in it. Dadoes are cut on a table saw using multiple cuts with a regular blade, or one cut with a dado head. Router and shaper cutters are available for the same purpose.

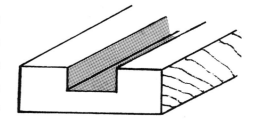

FACE FRAME—The finished surface boards of a cabinet. Doors are hung from a face frame, either inside the frame edges or lapped over the frame, depending on the hardware used.

See drawing on page 27.

MORTISE—A cut made with a chisel or router to remove a volume of wood necessary to receive another component such as a tenon; also used to describe the cut made to receive the hinges on the fly box.

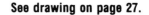
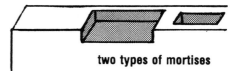

two types of mortises

PLOUGH—A groove cut exactly the same way as a dado. The difference being that ploughs (or plows) are cut parallel to the grain.

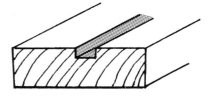

RABBET—A right angle cut made from the surface to an edge of a board. In the case of an edge rabbet joint, one of the rabbet dimensions is the same as the thickness of the adjoining piece, and the other dimension (depth) is variable.

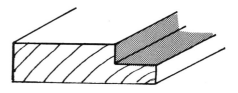

RAIL—The horizontal member of a face frame.

See drawing on page 27.

ROUND-OVER—A self-descriptive term used to describe a molding cut. See cove for machining.

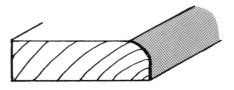

SPLINE—A piece, often made of plywood, inserted into the grooves of two members to align and strengthen a joint. The groove width is equal to the spline thickness which is normally about a third of the width of the members joined.

STILES—The vertical members of a face frame into which the rails abut. The Headquarters plan shows the stiles notched to receive rails, which is just one of many joints that could be used.

See drawing on page 27.

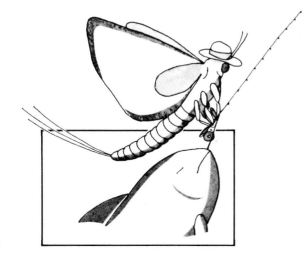

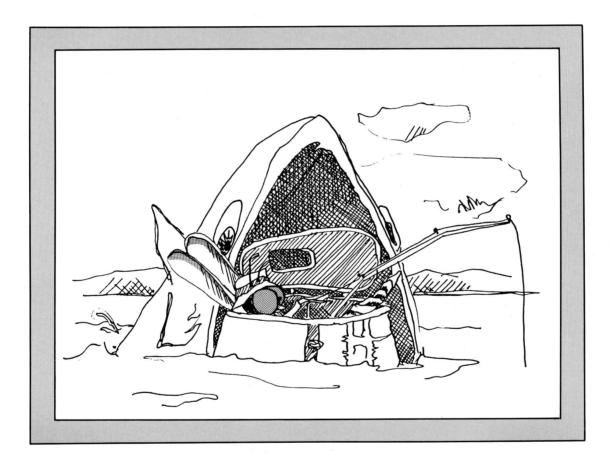